Original publication: "Hudební nauka Klíček 2"
Author: Eva Šašinková, M.M., Ph.D., M.B.A.
Illustrations: Mgr. Kateřina Kovářová
Original graphic design: Lumír Kaděra
Original publisher: Czech Music Edition, Prague, Czech Republic, 2022
Website: www.hudebni-publikace.cz
Copyright: Eva Šašinková, M.M., Ph.D., M.B.A.
Original Czech version ISBN: 978-80-907578-8-2

English adaptation: "Clefi's Music Notebook 2"
Illustrations: Mgr. Kateřina Kovářová
Translation, adaptation, and graphic design: Roman Placzek, D.M.A.
Publisher: BumbleBeeNotes™ Music Publishing, Manlius, NY, USA, 2025
Catalog number: cbbn002-wb-007
Website: www.bumblebeenotes.com
Copyright: BumbleBee Notes™ Inc. Music Corporation
ISBN: 979-8-9919035-6-1

Clefi's Little Crossword Review

Across:

5. The treble clef.
8. A four-beat note.
9. A combination of three or more notes.
12. Small sections of musical notation.
13. The distance between E and F.
16. The names of tone and notes.
17. The canceling accidental.
18. The difference between two pitches.
19. The altered note F.
21. The vertical line attached to shorter notes.
22. F clef.
24. The line connecting several eighth notes.

Down:

1. A part off an eight note.
2. The distance between C and D.
3. The one-beat rest.
4. C4.
6. The primary scale.
7. Musical symbols for tones.
10. The grid used for musical notation.
11. The major scale with the most sharps.
14. The four parts of the musical staff.
15. A two-beat note.
20. Musical symbols for silence in music.
23. The five parts of the musical staff.

Eva Šašinková, M.M., Ph.D., MBA, the author of the series, lives in Prague, Czech Republic, where she concertizes and holds academic positions at the Pilsen Conservatory and Academy of Music in Prague. Since childhood, Eva has dreamed of becoming a music teacher, sharing her passion and experience of love for music, especially with children. She has a deep love for the double bass, her instrument, in which she holds a master's degree. However, Eva also profoundly admires the piano, an instrument that was an inseparable part of her

About the Author

childhood. This admiration is the reason behind the concept of her method, which she based on the keyboard's layout. Eva is convinced that the piano is a unique instrument designed to help explain the fundamentals of music theory, the meaning of tones and melody, and the mission of music. She successfully proves her firm conviction in the practical application of her method. The story of her project started with a children's story that came to life during a trying period in the author's life.

Her passion for teaching children and desire to share her knowledge helped her concentrate on the essentials. During her pedagogical activities, Eva noticed that the materials available to her for the curriculum presentation were not, in her professional opinion, satisfactory. She started to visit music schools in her home country, the Czech Republic, comparing, editing, reworking, and creating. As a result, Eva began to bring worksheets filled with information and fun activities to the music education classes to make students' time learning music theory more engaging, easily accessible, and entertaining. The reactions of the young music students and fellow pedagogues were overwhelmingly positive.

Professor Eva managed to engage children's senses from all angles—drawing, singing, and practical demonstrations on a keyboard—everything children appreciated. On top of that, she had "The Story of a Song, "which kicked off a star career for one little boy, Clefi. He welcomes children in his "Clefi's Little Notebook" and helps them learn more in the four volumes of his "Clefi's Music Notebook." He plays and sings with them in "Clefi's Little Music Education Notebook" (in the translated version integrated into "Clefi's Little Notebook" – editor's note) and "Clefi's Musical Instruments" written for little musicians. Clefi helps them practice their newly acquired knowledge in three workbooks full of fun tasks and exercises. Children play with little Clefi, learn, and get ready for the more dedicated encounter with Lady Music and their chosen instrument in a fun and engaging way. And maybe it will become the love of their lives, their calling, and a hobby, as it happened to the author.

And to the sad faces of those who did not have the luck to learn from the best teachers and publications and did not have the best ... va says with her clever little smile: "If you ... n open heart, the muse will not ask you ... will kiss you on the brow when you least ... it and be ready!"

Author's Foreword

Clefi's New Music Education School is a unified music education method for children, amateur musicians, and music students.

Based on my extensive multi-genre musical performing career, many years of experience teaching children, and my terminal education degree in music theory, I have created a unified music education program for children from an early age to young musicians who choose to study music more seriously. The New Music Education School leans on children's natural perception of music. It offers young musicians and their teachers a unified educational system of fundamental music theory aiming to support musical creativity. Its main goal is to awaken children's musicianship based on creativity and the ability to sing a song, play it on a musical instrument of their choice, and write it down correctly, the sort of musicianship that enables them to use their musical knowledge theoretically and practically.

The first book, Clefi's Little Notebook, is tailored for the youngest musicians. It introduces us to Clefi, a charming little boy who shares his story. Clefi becomes our companion on this musical adventure. In Clefi's Little Notebook, children delve into musical notation, the birth of a song, a musical note, a musical staff, a clef (which inspired Clefi's name), the musical alphabet, and a scale. They learn to read and write notes in the fourth, the middle octave, and practice their new skills through exercises, puzzles, engaging tasks, and songs they play and sing.

Clefi's Music Notebooks 1, 2, 3, and **4** follow Clefi's Little Notebook. These four full-color music textbooks stand out for their unique conceptual design. Each volume is a complete unit and can be used individually.

At the same time, all four volumes are designed as one method, seamlessly following one another, so that the children can acquire a complete knowledge of the fundamentals of music theory in a friendly and engaging way.

Beautiful illustrations and graphic design enhance the unique quality of these lovely publications. All textbooks are suitable for children, amateur musicians, and professional music students.

This music education series explains the fundamentals of music theory quickly and efficiently so that children can understand and practice them while playing musical instruments, singing, and harmonizing. The textbooks aim to develop children's musical abilities, aural skills, perception of tone pitch and duration, and rhythmical and tonal melodic structure.

The idea behind this methodological concept is to make children first listen, then understand, learn, utilize, and create. When born, a baby listens and absorbs speech. When it understands it, it tries to pronounce the first words. A child attempts to understand the connections and context. Only after several years can a child logically think and systematically create. And the same applies to the understanding of music! What would the knowledge of music theory be for if we did not listen to music and didn't use the ingenious system of music theory in practice? However, the same applies both ways. How can we expect to evolve in our music-making if we refuse to learn and explore the mysteries of music, its tonal relations, harmony, and rhythm?

This method will help children fully absorb music and learn essential human and life values through it. We can learn to read and write only if we listen to our parents talk from an early age. Then, we learn the words, pronounce them, and understand their meaning. The same applies to music and how we understand it.

I hope my books will bring you joy and help many young musicians open the door to the beautiful world of music.

Eva 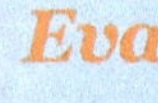

What's Inside:

Similar to "Clefi's Little Notebook," this book presents a collection of enchanting folk songs from the rich Czech folklore tradition, designed for music education. To accurately utilize their intended purpose, each song requires accurate adaptation and translation into English, which would take up more space than these volumes can accommodate without disrupting their intended design. Therefore, we are offering a standalone "Clefi & Notelina's Songbook," featuring all the songs from all nine volumes of Clefi's New Music Education School series, along with accurately and sensibly translated and adapted English lyrics.

Dear musical friends,

In this volume of our notebooks, we invite you to embark on a journey through music into space. Why space? The answer is simple: music is otherworldly and timeless. Furthermore, Czech and American music share a significant historical connection. In 1969, American astronauts Neil Armstrong and Buzz Aldrin, part of the Apollo 11 mission, became the first people to walk on the moon. For this monumental flight, Neil Armstrong selected a piece that had resonated with him since his days playing in a university symphony orchestra. The piece he chose to play on the moon was the New World Symphony, composed by Antonín Dvořák, a Bohemian composer who served as the director of the New York Conservatory from 1892 to 1895.

To perform works like the renowned New World Symphony, it's essential for us to not only become skilled instrumentalists but also to grasp the nuances of musical notation. That's why we will delve deeper into music and further uncover its incredible mysteries.

In this Notebook, we will explain the pitch class system and learn more about scales. We will discover the differences between major and minor scales, learn how to use the circle of fifths to create all the major scales with sharps and flats. We will learn about intervals and create fifth chords and their inversions. We will talk about chord symbols, which we will need later on when creating harmonic accompaniment. We will also learn about tempo markings, repetitions, upbeats, octave transpositions, syncopes, and triplets.

At the end of the book, we will travel back in time to uncover the origins and evolution of the minor scale. We will explore why we use three forms of the minor scale today: natural, harmonic, and melodic. Additionally, we will read about the famous Greek scholar Pythagoras, who studied tones and discovered the principles that influence their pitch. His work laid the foundation for the theory of tuning and intervals.

Throughout this journey, we will come to understand that everything has its significance, its own laws, and its mysterious beauty, much like the universe itself. We look forward to spending this time together as we uncover more secrets of music.

Yours,
Clefi and Notelina

MUSICAL NOTATION

NOTES are **musical symbols** for **tones**. Tones are musical sounds. Note's **shape** determines its **duration**.

RESTS are **musical symbols** for **silence in music**. Rest's **shape** determines its **duration**.

MUSICAL STAFF has five lines and four spaces counted from the bottom up.

Ledger Lines

To accommodate a wider range of music marked on one musical staff, we use additional lines below and above the staff called ledger lines. Ledger lines are short vertical lines assigned to each individual note outside the main staff range. The spacing must correspond with the spacing of the main staff.

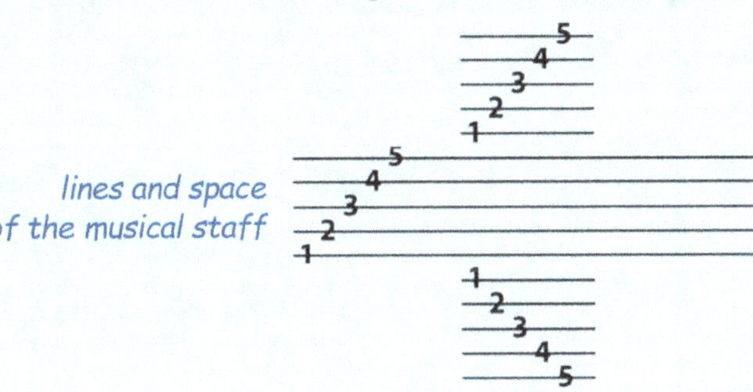

Notes on the Musical Staff

Notes can be positioned either **on the lines** of the staff or **in its spaces**. When a note with a stem is located below the middle line of the staff, the stem extends upward on the right side. Conversely, notes placed above the middle line have their stems pointing downward on the left side.

CLEFS

A clef is a musical symbol determining **the pitch of the notes within the staff**. It's always placed at the beginning of the staff. Clefs are named by the pitch range and their determining tone. Treble and bass clefs are the most common clefs used today.

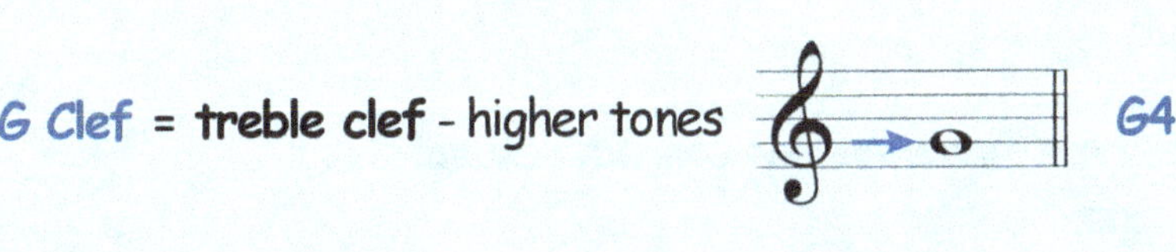

E Circle the right examples of the musical notation and cross out the wrong ones.

NOTES & RESTS

DURATION OF NOTES AND RESTS

Notes and rests have **different names** and various **numbers of beats**. The names of notes and rests are given by their ratio related to the duration of the 4/4 measure, which is also known as the **complete** or **whole** measure." (For example, we can fit eight **"eighth notes"** into one 4/4 measure).

One whole C or 4/4 measure = 1 whole note = 2 half notes = 4 quarter notes = 8 eighth notes...

	NOTES	RESTS	
whole	o	▬	**4** beats
half	♩	▬	**2** beats
quarter	♩	𝄽	**1** beat
eighth	♪	𝄾	**1/2** beat
sixteenth	♬	𝄿	**1/4** beat

FLAGS & BEAMS

Eighth notes and notes of shorter values have **flags**. We can connect several short notes by using **beams**. **Beams replace flags**.
The number of beams must be the same as the number of flags.
Example: sixteenth notes have two flags, so connected sixteenth notes must have two beams.

DOT AFTER NOTE

A dot after a note extends the notes duration by the half off its duration.
Example: a half note = 2 beats - dotted half note = 3 beats (2 + 1)

E Copy the notes and rests into empty measures, then write their names in the spaces below.

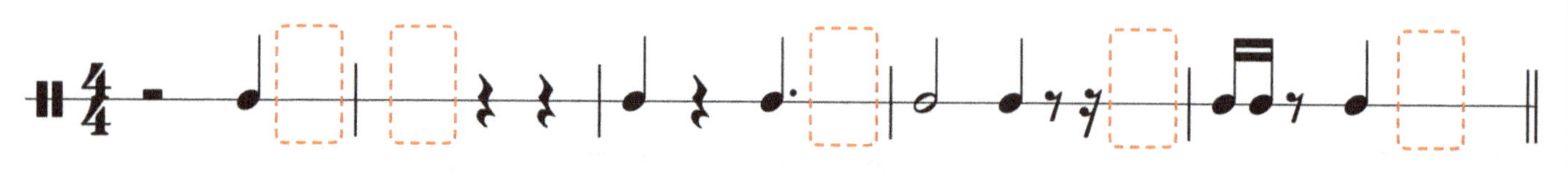

ACCIDENTALS

PRIMARY TONE ROW

The **primary tone row** has seven tones: C, D, E, F, G, A, and B. These tones repeat in the same exact order at different pitches. Some tones are a step and some are a half-step apart.

A **half-step** is the smallest difference between two tones. A **step** consists of two half-steps.

If we wish to **raise** or **lower the pitch** of any of the primary tones, we use **accidentals**.

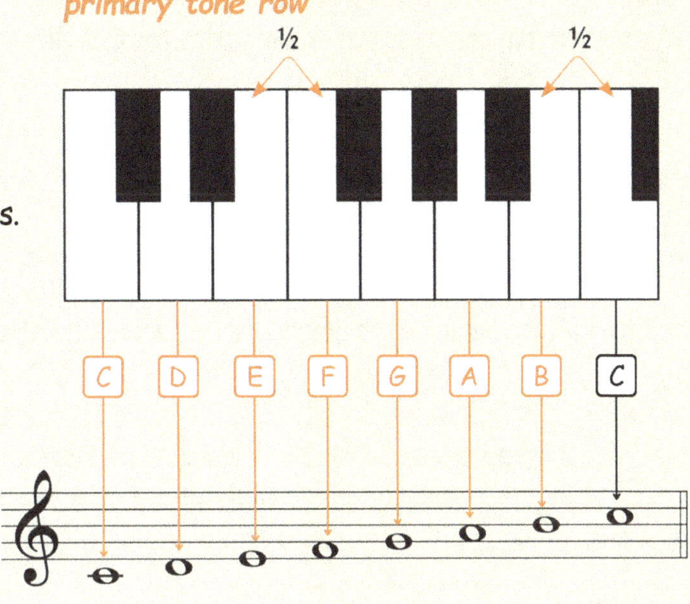

ACCIDENTALS

Accidentals are musical symbols used to alter - **raise** or **lower** - the pitch of tones in the musical notation. Accidentals are placed in front of the tone we wish to alter. Free-standing accidentals alter all the same-named notes from the one to which they are applied until the end of the measure.

- SHARPS **raise** a note by a **half-step**. The symbol **#** or the word **"sharp"** is added after the altered note's name.
- FLATS **lower** a note by a **half-step**. The symbol *b* or the word **"flat"** is added after the altered note's name.
- NATURALS **cancel** previously imposed **sharps** and **flats**.

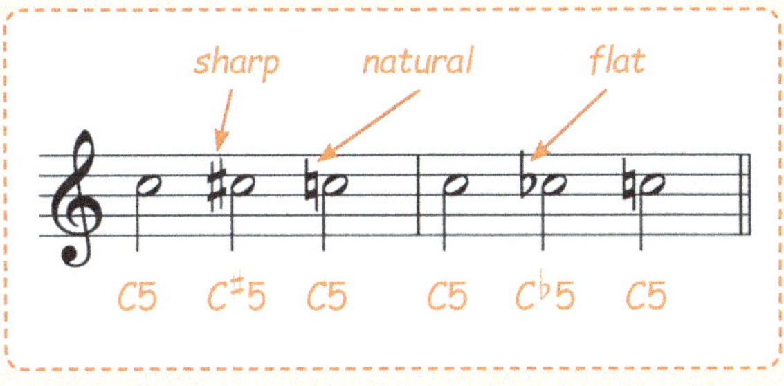

DOUBLE ACCIDENTALS

- DOUBLE SHARPS **raise** a note by **two half-steps**. The symbol **X** or the words **"double sharp"** are added after the altered note's name.
- DOUBLE FLATS **lower** a note by **two half-steps**. The symbol *bb* or the words **"double flat"** are added after the altered note's name.

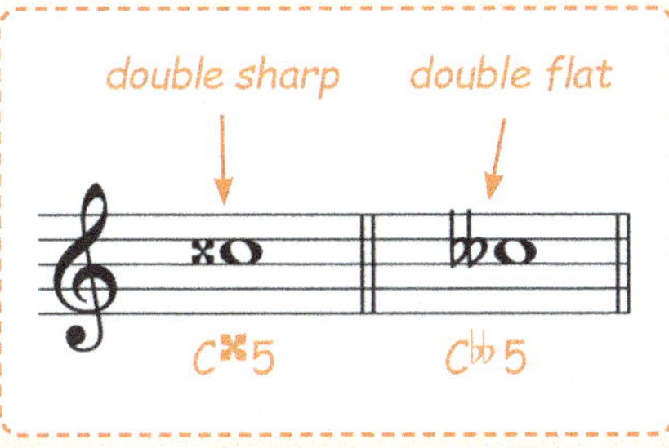

E Write in the half notes according to their names below the staff.

MAJOR SCALES

SCALE is a row of tones organized by preset rules.
Major and **minor** scales are the most common scales used in wester music.

MAJOR SCALES

- C MAJOR is the **primary major scale**: C D E F G A B C. It consists of the tones of the primary tone row.

- We can build a major scale from any other tone - primary or altered. The only thing necessary is to observe the **step and half-step structure** of the major scale. To accommodate this rule, we have to **alter** - raise or lower - some notes when starting from any other note than "C."

- The step structure of the major scale is: | 1 | 1 | 1/2 | 1 | 1 | 1 | 1/2 |

- The major scales for which we **raise** some notes to build a major scale are called **major scales with sharps**. The major scales for which we **lower** some notes to build a major scale are called **major scales with flats**.

MAJOR SCALES WITH SHARPS

- Major scales with sharps originate from the C major scale, building upon **the fifth** (the fifth step) of the preceding scale.
- The foundational scale, **C major**, has no key signature, meaning it **has no sharps** or **flats**.
- Each following scale begins on the fifth (the fifth degree) of the previous scale and includes **one additional sharp**, which is always applied to its **seventh degree**.
- The diagram of the origin and progression of major scales is known as The Circle of Fifths.
- The sharps are added in the following order:
  F#, C#, G#, D#, A#, E#, and B#.

- The scales with sharps are:
  G major, D major, A, major,
  E major, F# major and C# major.

| E | Copy the sharps according the example.

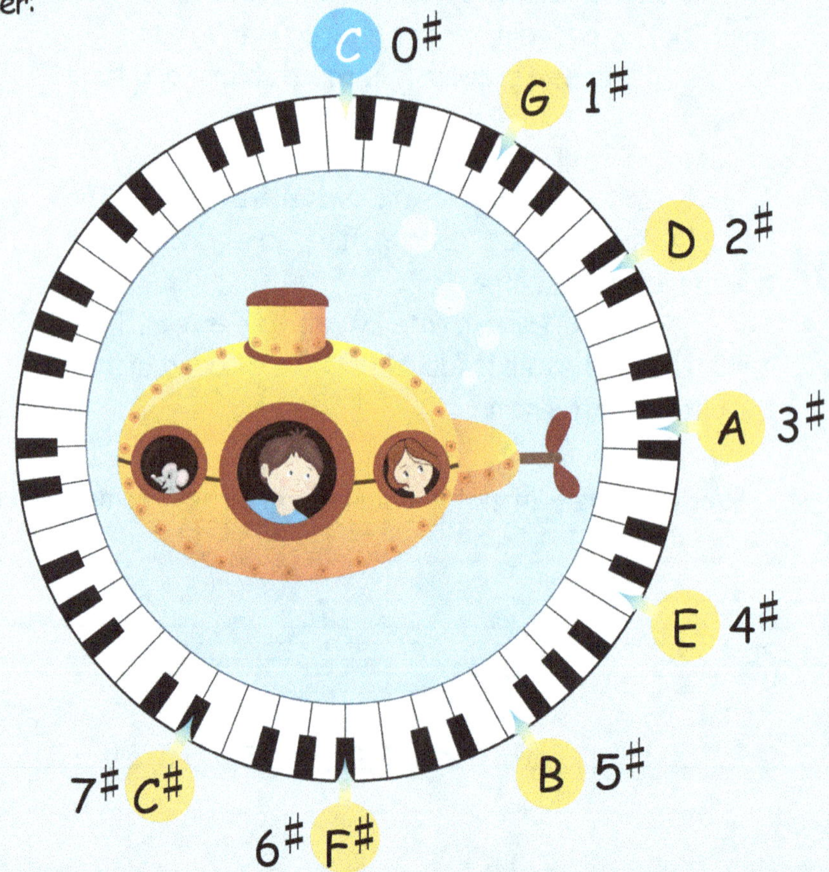

SCALES WITH 5, 6, AND 7 SHARPS

In *Clefi's Music Notebook 1* we mastered the major scales up to **four sharps**:
G major (1#), **D major** (2#), **A major** (3#), and **E major** (4#).
The remaining major scales with sharps are:
B major (5#), **F sharp major** (6#), and **C sharp major** (7#).

B major
- key signature - 5 sharps - F#, C#, G#, D#, and A#
- the major scales with sharps: G, D, A, E, **B**, F#, C#

The new sharps are always added to the seventh step (degree).

F# major
- key signature - 6 sharps - F#, C#, G#, D#, A#, and E#
- the major scales with sharps: G, D, A, E, B, **F#**, C#

C# major
- key signature - 7 sharps - F#, C#, G#, D#, A#, E#, and B#
- the major scales with sharps: G, D, A, E, B, F#, **C#**

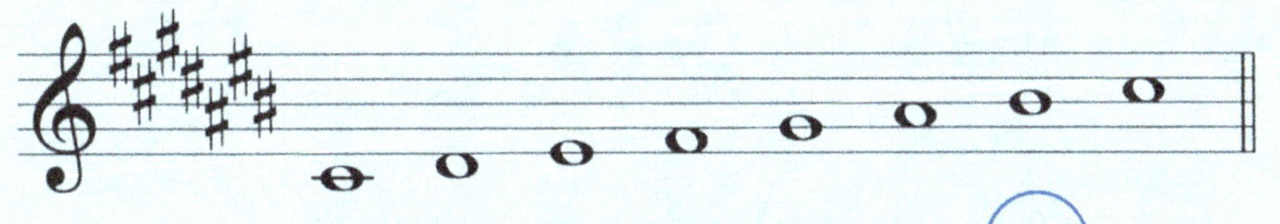

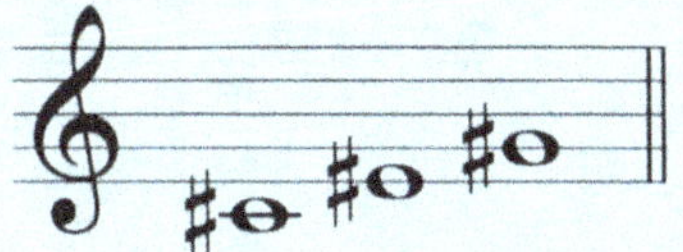

A major scale can be divided into two equal parts - tetrachords.
Two consecutive major scales share one tetrachord.

The 1st tetrachord starts on the scale's keynote   *The 2nd tetrachord ends on the scale's keynote*

B major: B   C#   D#   E   F#   G#   A#   B

F# major: F#   G#   A#   B   C#   D#   E#   F#

C# major: C#   D#   E#   F#   G#   A#   B#   C#

REVIEW 1

Learn to play or sing the melody of this beautiful Moravian folk song (*Moravia is the eastern region of the Czech Republic*) about a cold stream and fond memories.

Clefi & Notelina's Songbook, pg. 63

E Using correct key signatures transpose the first five measures of the song above to the keys of B major and C# major.

B major

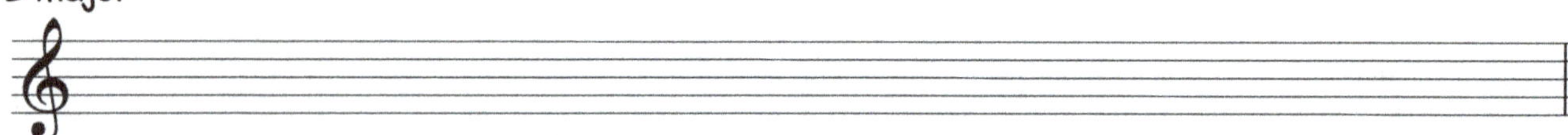

C# major

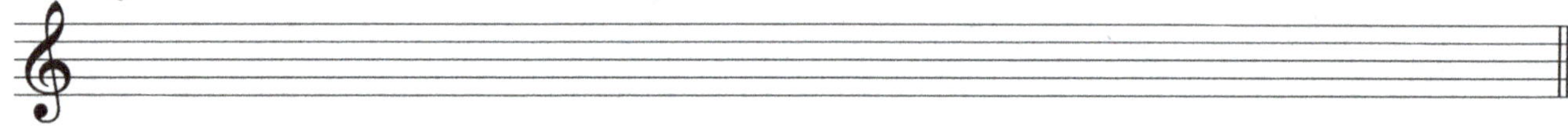

E Review the reading notes in the bass clef. Write the names of the notes on the dotted line beneath the staff, and then transpose that section of the song to C♯ major.

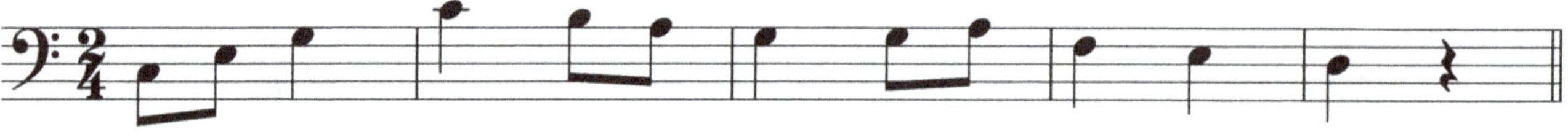

C# major

E "I'm Not Going to the Forest" begins with a major melodic fifth chord. From the root tone, identify and mark the key and the key signature for all three openings.

Clefi & Notelina's Songbook, pg. 35

E Fill the table with all the major scales with sharps. Indicate their names, number of sharps, and the names of the notes making their tonic fifth chord.

scale's name	number of sharps	tonic fifth chord		
C major	0	C	E	G
	1	G		
			F#	
				E

E Identify the keys of the songs by their first two measures. Do you know all the songs? You can find all of them in *Clefi & Notelina's Songbook.*

E Subsequent major scales share one tetrachord. Carefully examine the tetrachords below and write down the scale to which they belong as the first and second tetrachord.

is the first tetrachord of the .... major scale.

and the second tetrachord of the .... major scale.

is the first tetrachord of the .... major scale.

and the second tetrachord of the .... major scale.

INTERVALS

INTERVALS

A musical **interval** is the difference or distance between the pitches of two tones.
- The distance is measured from the origination tone, the lower tone of the interval, to the upper, the destination tone.
- The fundamental intervals are: Unison, Second, Third, Fourth, Fifth, Sixth, Seventh, and Octave.
- Intervals are marked using the numbers: Unison - 1, Second - 2, Third - 3, etc.

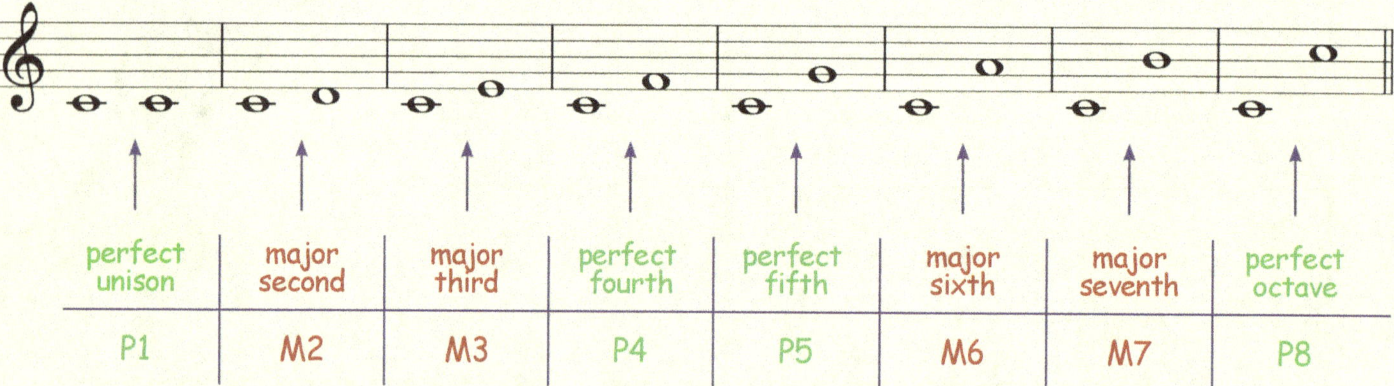

PRIMARY AND DERIVED INTERVALS

Intervals are divided into **primary** and **derived**.
- **Primary intervals** are the intervals contained within a major scale calculated from the tonic (the origination tone) and all the tones of the scale including the tonic itself *(see the diagram above)*.
- **Derived intervals** are altered primary intervals. The intervals can be augmented (enlarged) or diminished (shrunk). We create them by altering one of the tones of a primary interval.
  For example:
  C - G = perfect fifth is the primary interval.
  C - G# = augmented fifth is the derived interval.

PRIMARY INTERVALS

Primary intervals are divided into **perfect** and **major**.
- The perfect intervals are **unison - P1**, **fourth - P4**, **fifth - P5**, and **octave - P8**. We mark them using the letter "P."
- The major intervals are **second - M2**, **third - M3**, **sixth - M6**, and **seventh - M7**. We mark them using the letter "M."

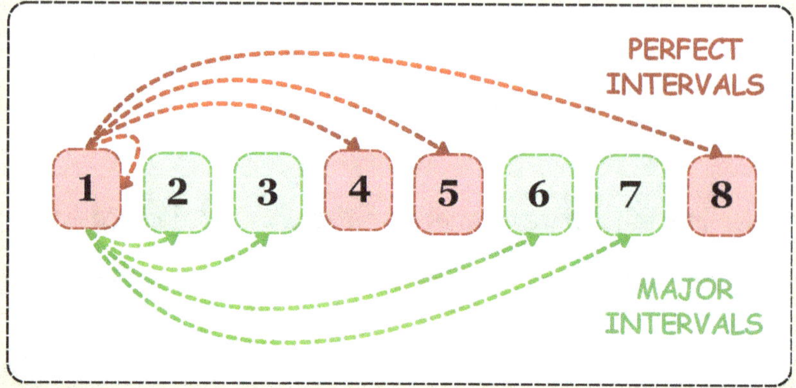

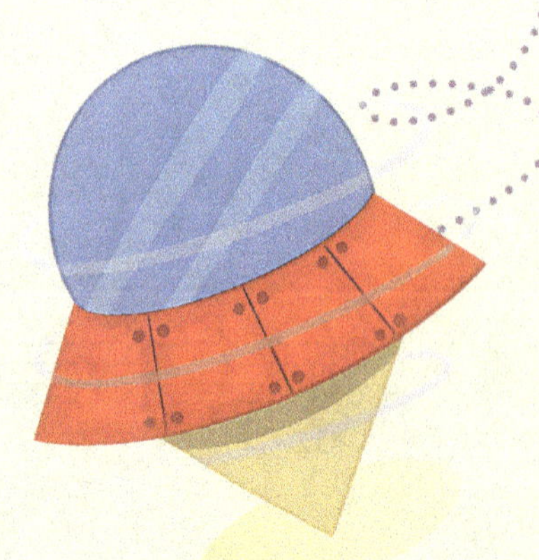

Primary intervals can be created in two ways:
by counting the **number of half-steps** or from a **major scale**.

- Each interval is characterized by **a given number of half-steps** between the two notes.

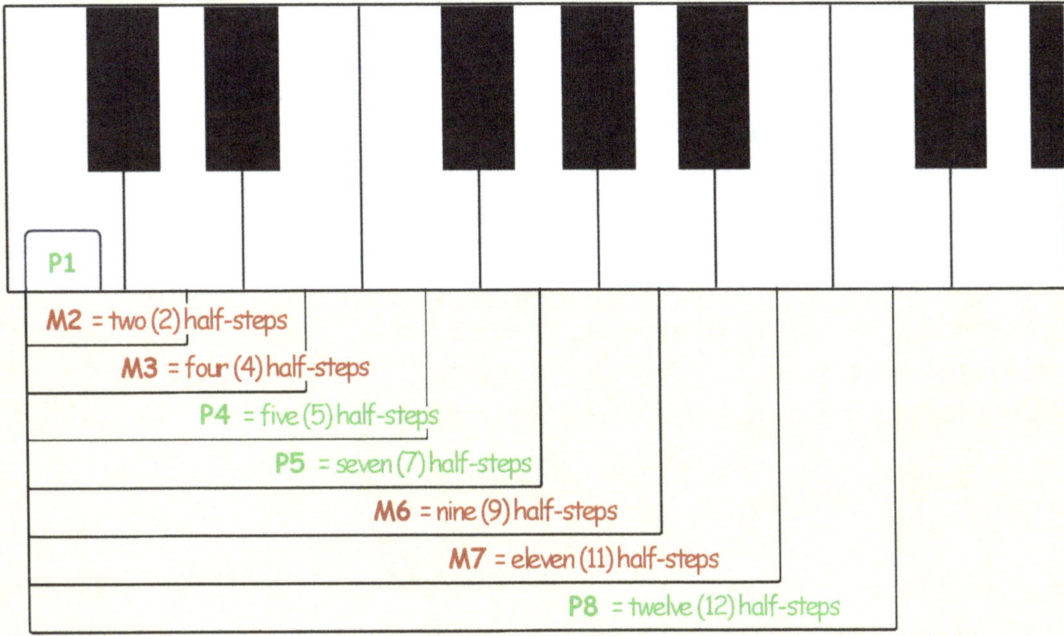

- **Primary intervals** are those **between the tonic** and **all other tones of a major scale**. If we need to create a primary interval from a given tone, we can simply build a major scale from it and count the desired interval.

EXAMPLE

Let's find M3 from the tone D up.
1. *Build the D major scale (2#s = F# and C#).*
2. *The third tone of the D major scale is F#.*
3. *The M3 (major third) from D up is D - F#.*

D	E	F#	G	A	B	C#	D
1	2	3	4	5	6	7	8

E | Fill in the notes according to the intervals named above the staves.

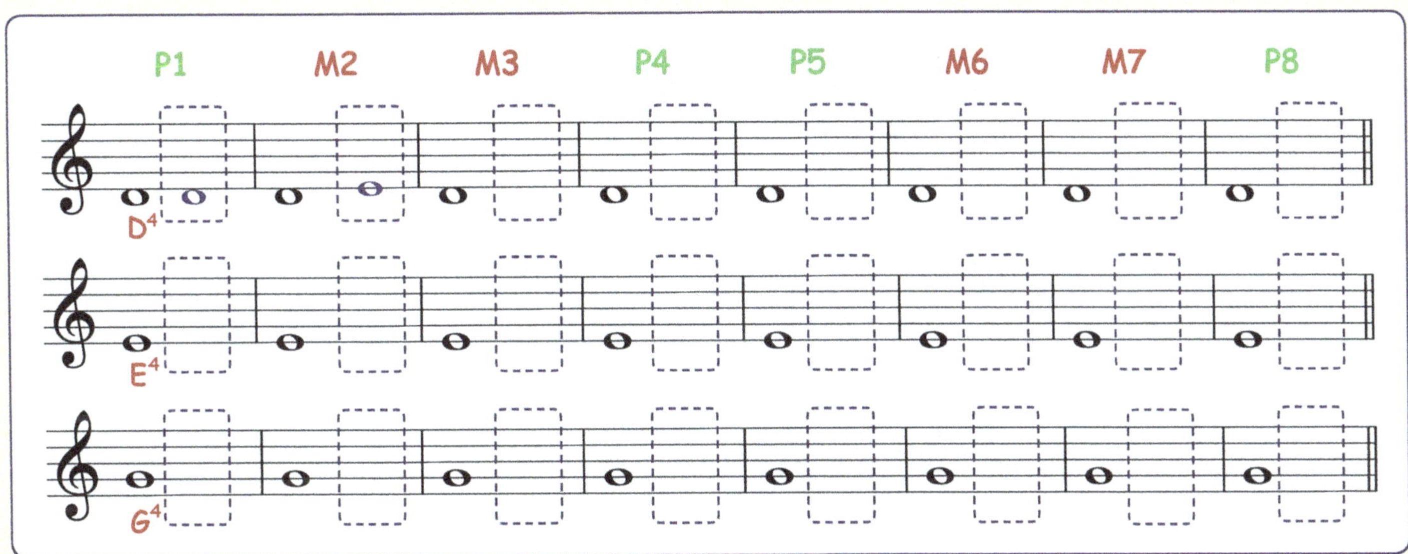

PERFECT INTERVALS

PERFECT INTERVALS

Perfect intervals are the **primary intervals**.
Perfect intervals are the unison, fourth, fifth, and octave.

The name of these intervals is derived from their character and use. These intervals do not have other variations like the major and minor intervals. They are considered highly consonant (pleasant to human ears) and stable intervals. They are also used for the tuning of string instruments - harmonics (tones produced by a string after a light touch of a finger) are produced only in these perfect intervals.

Perfect intervals serve us well for tuning musical instruments by ear.

To determine the perfect intervals from any tone, all we have to do is build a major scale from the chosen tone up and listen to the pitch differences between the steps 1-1, 1-4, 1-5, and 1-8.

If we decide to increase or decrease the size of the perfect intervals by a half-step, we create altered intervals called augmented (enlarged) or diminished (decreased).

Examples from the tone C4.

E Write the correct notes into the frames next to the root notes. Learn the songs starting with the perfect intervals from page 11. In songs 2 and 3, circle all P4 in blue and all P5 in red.

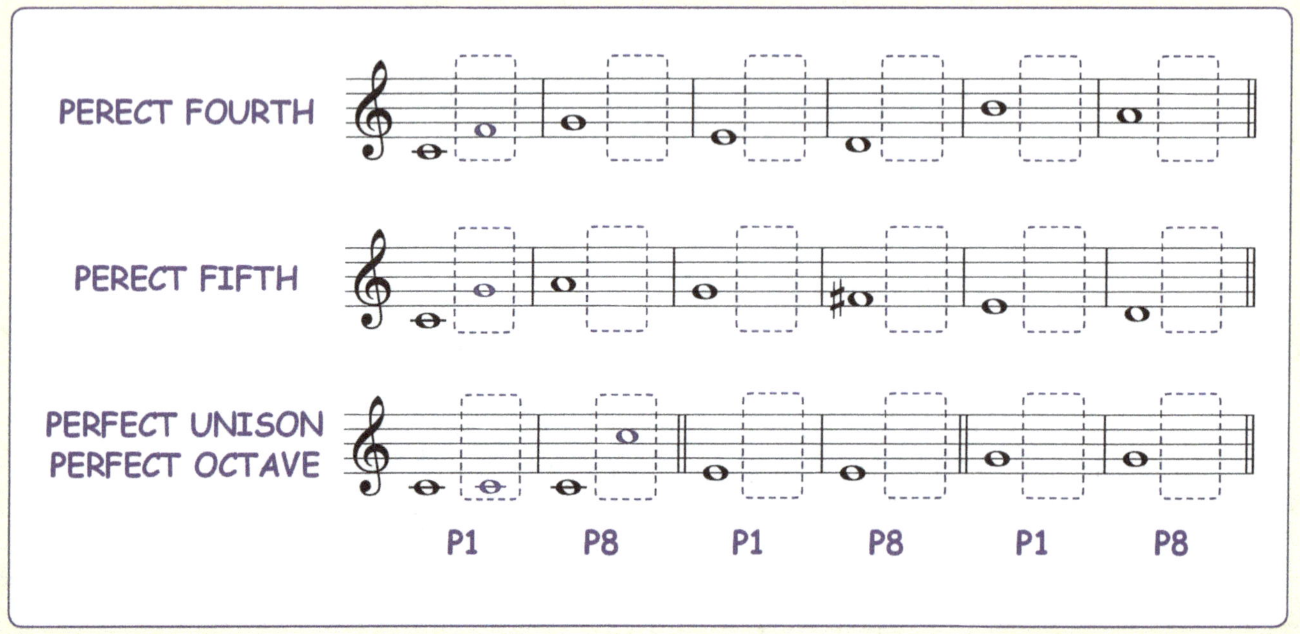

PERFECT UNISON

Clefi & Notelina's Songbook, pg. 61
Moonlight and Starllight
P1

PERFECT FOURTH

Clefi & Notelina's Songbook, pg. 64
It's Just Me, Only Me
P4
1.
2.

PERFECT FOURTH

Clefi & Notelina's Songbook, pg. 67
Farewell, Farewell
P5

PERFECT FIFTH

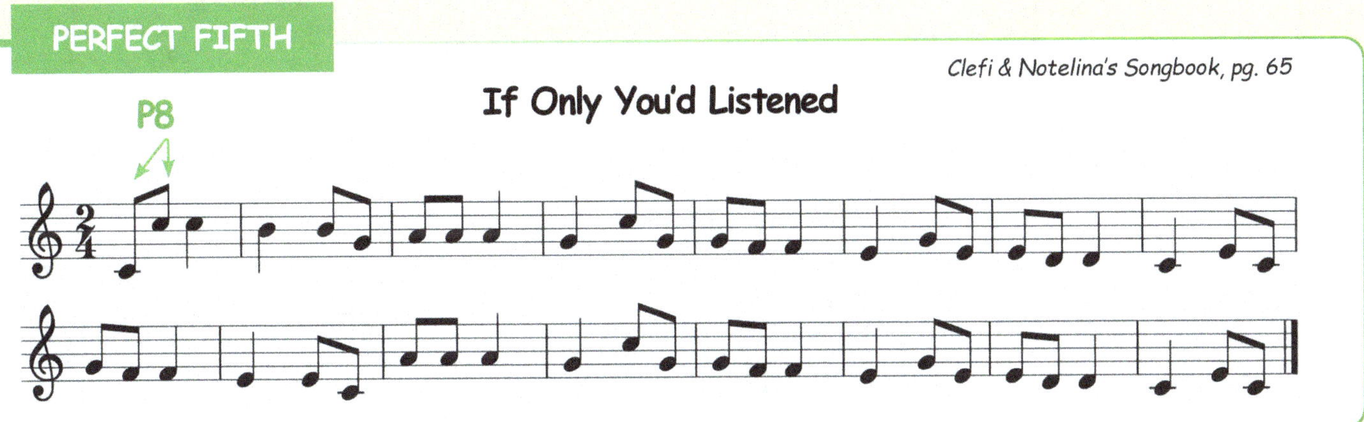
Clefi & Notelina's Songbook, pg. 65
If Only You'd Listened
P8

MAJOR & MINOR INTERVALS

MAJOR INTERVALS

- Major intervals are the **primary intervals**.
- Major intervals are the second, third, sixth, and seventh.
- Major intervals are not as stable as the perfect ones, they have their **minor** siblings.
- Major (primary) intervals are created similarly to the perfect intervals - using the major scale.

MINOR INTERVALS

- Minor intervals are considered **altered intervals**.
- In music, they have the same importance as their major siblings.
- A minor interval is always a half-step smaller than the major one.

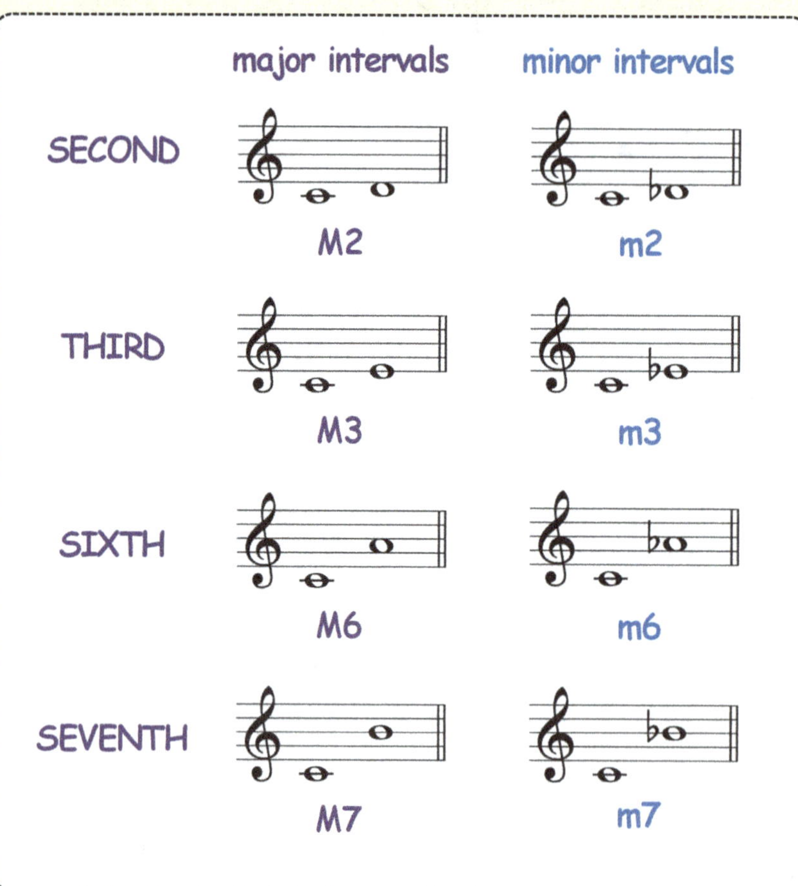

How to Create a Minor Interval

Let's find major and minor thirds from the note E4.

1. Build the major scale starting from E major = 4#: **F#, C#, G#, D#**.
2. The third tone of the scale is **G#**. The **major third is E - G#**.
3. **Lower** the third tone by a **half-step** to **G**. The **minor third is E - G**.

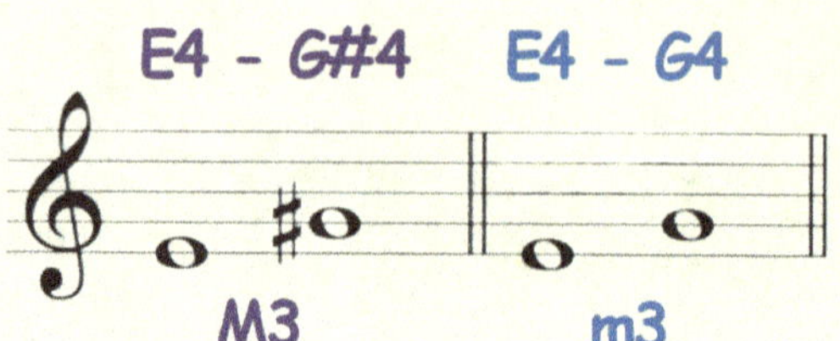

E   Fill in the notes according to the intervals named below the staff.

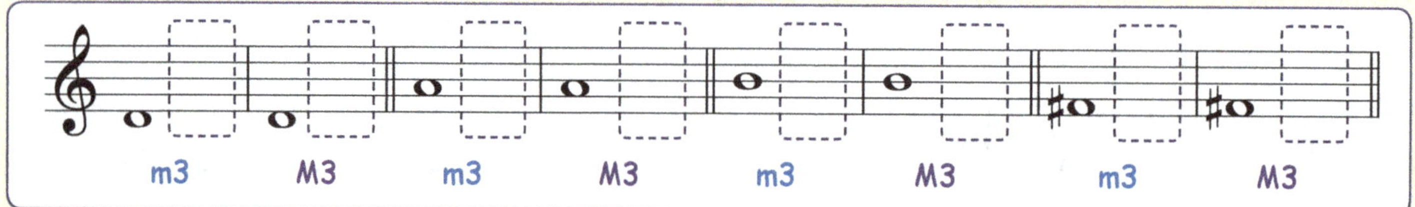

E Learn to identify both major and minor seconds and thirds, and then label all the intervals using abbreviated markings (M2, m2, M3, m3) to write them below the staves.

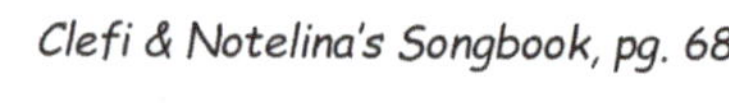

Oh, Meadow, Grass so Green

Sad Times Are Here

Cherish Me
and Care for Me, Mom

E Let's learn to recognize the M6, m6, and m7 intervals by ear. We will use the songs above as help. Write the names of the intervals on the dotted line below the measures.

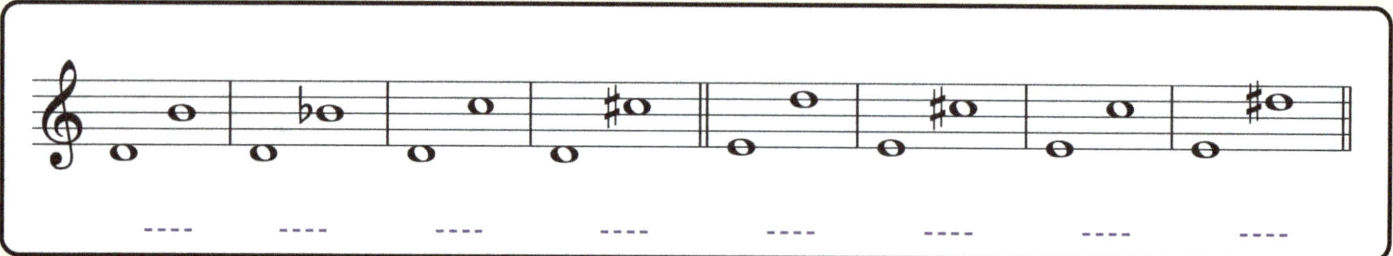

UPPER & LOWER INTERVALS

MELODIC INTERVAL = the second tone follows the root tone.
HARMONIC INTERVAL = both tones sound at the same time.

MELODIC INTERVALS

Melodic intervals can be divided into upper and lower.

- **Upper** melodic intervals are the intervals with **the root tone lower** then the second tone.(i.e. C4 - G4). All intervals crated between the root tone and the tones of the ascending C major scale are the **upper melodic perfect** and **major** (primary) **intervals**.

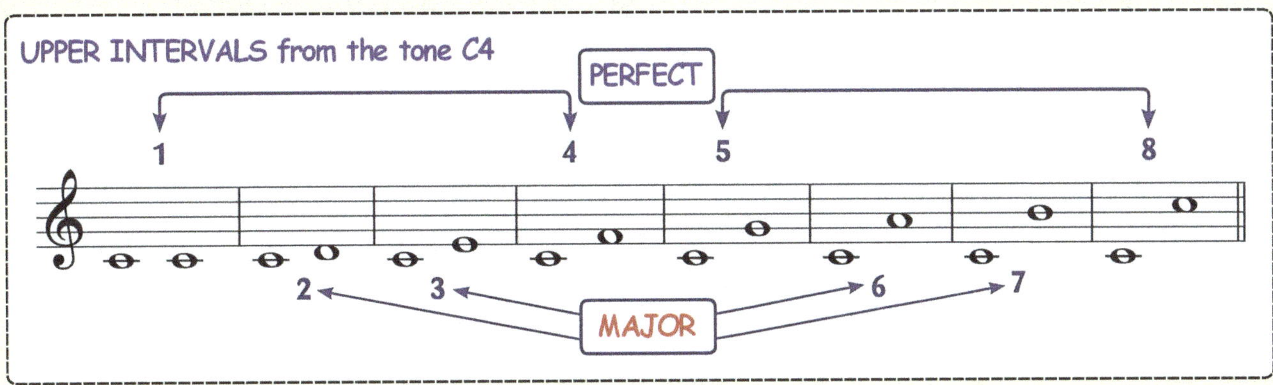

- **Lower** melodic intervals are the intervals with **the root tone higher** then the second tone (i.e. G4 - C4). All intervals crated between the root tone and the tones of the descending C major scale are the **lower melodic perfect** and **minor** intervals.

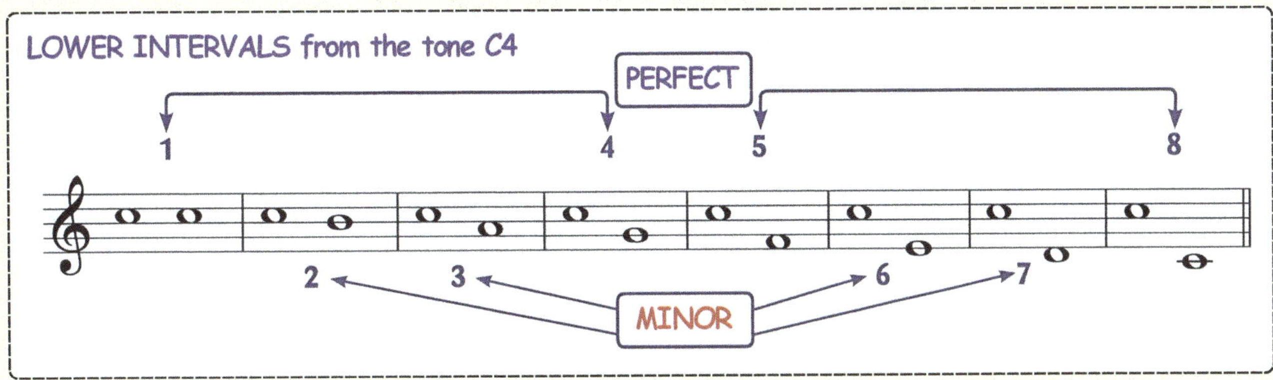

E The following opening measures of three songs start with the lower M2 interval.
Circle all lower M2 intervals you can find.

FIFTH CHORD (5) = the root position

The fifth chord is a **triad**. Its name is derived from the interval between the two outer tones - the interval of 5th. Inside the chord are two thirds, one on top of the other. A **tonic fifth chord** is built from the **root tone** (the **tonic** - the first tone) of a scale up. It's possible to change the order of the tones in the chord and create the fifth chord's **inversions**.

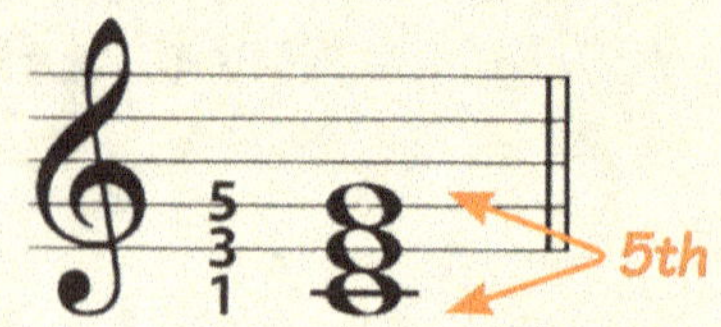

SIXTH CHORD (6) = the first inversion

If we take the root tone of a fifth chord and place it an octave higher (above the other two tones of the chord), we get the fifth chord's **first inversion**. It's called a **sixth chord** because now, the interval between the two outer tones of the new chord is the interval of 6th. The two inner intervals are 3rd on the bottom (the top 3rd of the initial fifth chord) and 4th on the top.

FOUR-SIXTH CHORD (6/4) = the second inversion

If we take the bottom note of a sixth chord and place it an octave higher (on top of the two other notes of the sixth chord), we get the fifth chord's **second inversion** called the **four-sixth chord**. It's called that because the interval between the two outer tones of the new chord is 6th and the bottom inner interval is the interval of 4th (the top inner interval of the sixth chord).

The chord inversions are marked with numbers:
Fifth chord = **5**; Sixth chord = **6**; Four-sixth chord = **6/4**.

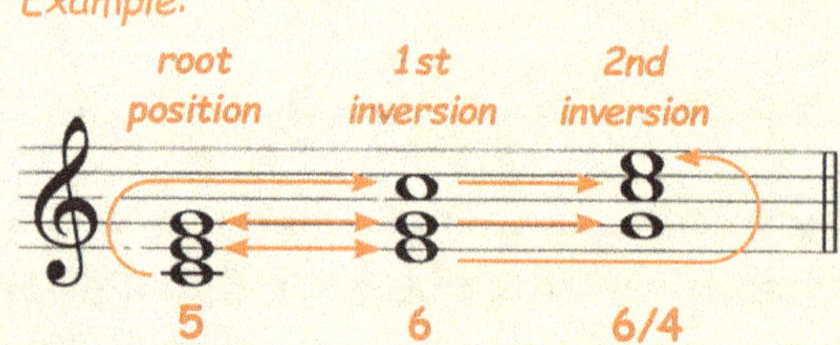

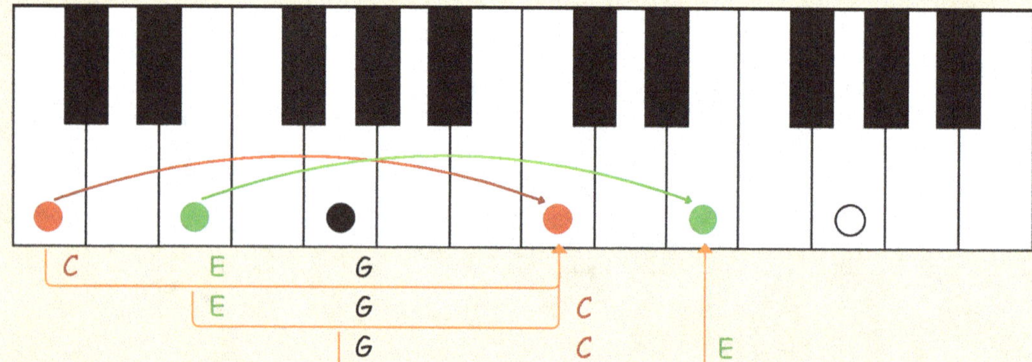

It's like moving pebbles assigned to a key on the keyboard from left to right.

E   Label the chords using correct numeric labels (5, 6, or 6/4).

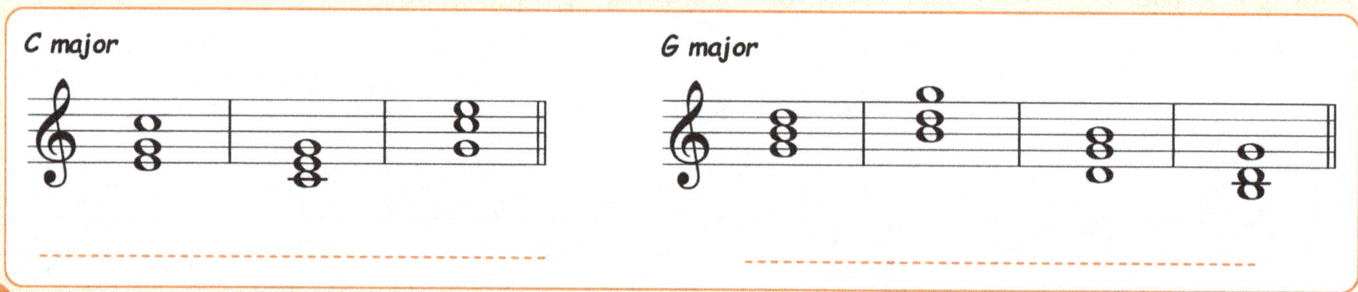

CHORD SYMBOLS

CHORD SYMBOLS

Chord symbols are **abbreviated labels for chords.** The major fifth chord is considered the primary chord. The chord symbol of the major fifth chord is the name of its root tone, the tonic in caapital letter. For example, the symbol of the C major fifth chord (C, E, G) is C.

> **CHORD SYMBOL CONTAINS**
> 1. **CHORD'S ROOT TONE**
> 2. **CHORD'S MODE**
> 3. **CHORD'S FORM & EXTENSIONS**

CHORD'S ROOT TONE

The chord's symbol is named after its **root tone.**
To determine the chord's root tone, we have to identify the **root position of the given chord** - the **tonic fifth chord.** The root position will have two 3rds on top of each other, and the outer tones of the triad will be 5th apart.

CHORD'S MODE

The mode of the chord describes its **character** or **mood**, which is generally either major or minor.

- The chords in a **major mode** have a **major 3rd** at the bottom of their root form. The chord symbol for chords in major mode is a capital letter. Example: C = C major chord = C-E-G.
- The chords in a **minor mode** have a **minor 3rd** at the bottom of its root form. The chord symbol for chords in minor mode is a capital letter with the suffix **-m** (*minore = Italian for minor*). Example: Cm = c minor chord = C-Eb-G.

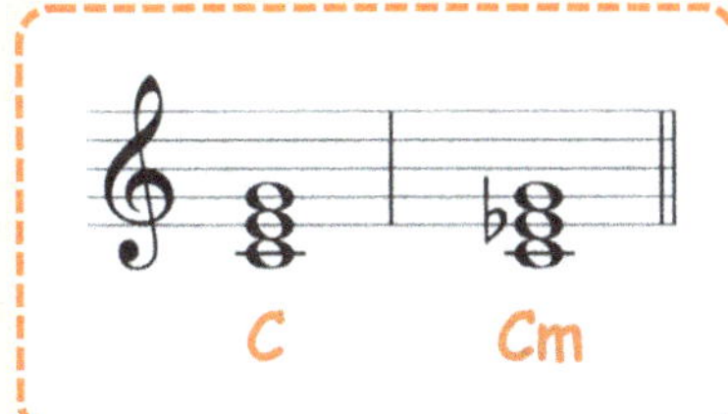

CHORD'S FORM and EXTENSIONS

The primary form of a chord is a **triad - three notes.** This form can be altered by changing of the triad notes pitches or by adding additional notes, extensions. Such alteration to the chord's primary form are marked by adding numbers to the chord symbol (C^7, C^{5+}).

Example:
- *number 7 = an added minor 7th = C^7 = C-E-G-Bb*
- *combination 5+ or 5# = augmented 5th = C^{5+} = C-E-G#*

SYMBOLS OF CHORD INVERSIONS

The chord inversions chord symbols have two letters separated by a forward slash - **the chord name/the lowest note.**

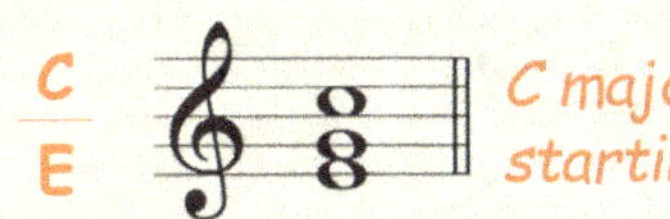

C major chord in the second inversion starting with E

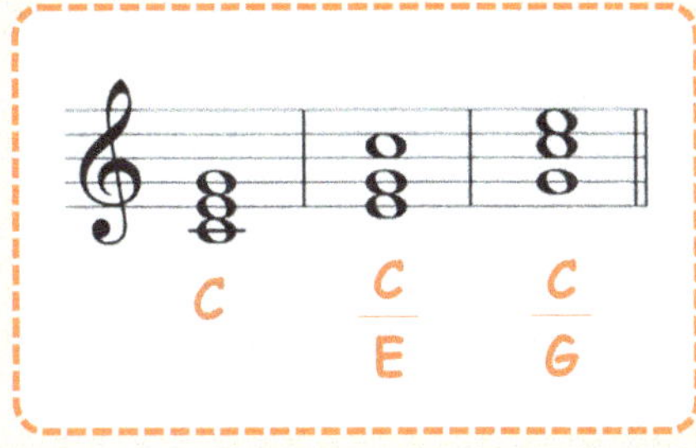

SCALE DEGREES

SCALE DEGREES

Steps in a scale are also called degrees and they are marked using roman numeral numbers:
I - one, **II** – two, **III** - three, **IV** - four, **V** - five, **VI** - six, **VII** - seven, **VIII** - eight.

Example using the C major scale:

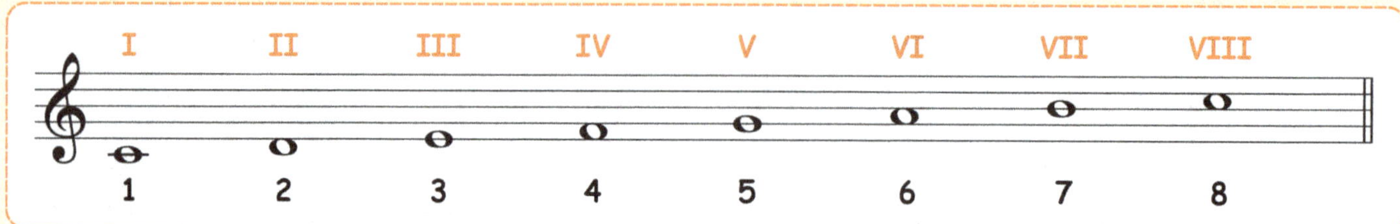

FUNDAMENTAL SCALE DEGREES

The fundamental scale degrees are:

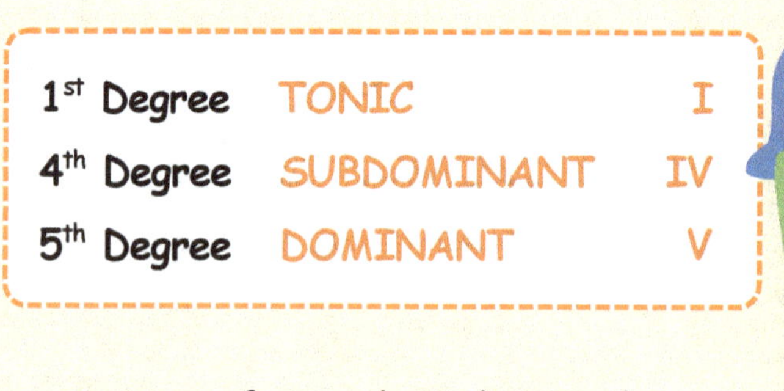

Tonic

The scale's 1ST degree, the **tonic**, is the corner stone of any scale. It dictates the tonality of a scale.

Dominant

The 5th degree, the **dominant**, is a very important degree of the scale.
It's called a "dominant" because of its strongest tendency to resolve into a tonic. It dominates to all other degrees of a scale.

Subdominant

The fourth degree, the **subdominant**, plays a crucial role within a musical scale by helping to establish its mode and tonality because of tis special relationship with the dominant. It earns its name for that relationship as well as its placement directly below the dominant (with "sub" meaning under or below).

LEADING TONE

The 7th scale degree plays a crucial melodic role as the leading tone. It creates melodic tension that seeks resolution into the 8th degree, which is identical to tonic. Additionally, as a part of the dominant chord (*a chord built on the scale's 5th degree*), it enhances its harmonic dominance.

HARMONIC FUNCTIONS

Harmonic functions are roles assigned to chords built from the tones of a scale on individual degrees.
The chords with the primary harmonic functions are those built on the fundamental scale degrees.
The fifth chords built on the fundamental degrees are described as:

- **T** - **tonic fifth chord** built of the 1st degree
- **S** - **subdominant fifth chord** built on the 4th degree
- **D** - **dominant fifth chord** built on the 5th degree

REVIEW 2

INTERVALS

E What song is this? A several quarter notes are missing. Fill in them according to the labels of the upper intervals, sing the tune, and identify the song.

Clefi & Notelina's Songbook, pg. 44

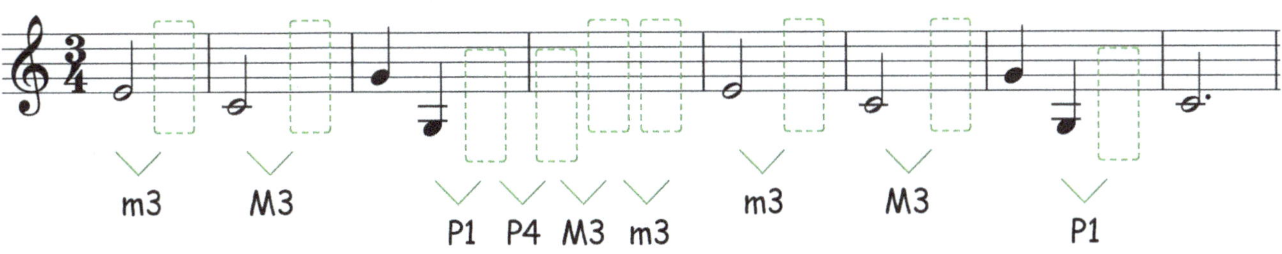

INVERSIONS OF FIFTH CHORDS AND CHORD SYMBOLS

E Label the chords by their correct position/inversion (5, 6, or 6/4).

E Notate fifth chords and their inversions according to the chord symbols (page 17).

HARMONIC FUNCTIONS

E Notate fifth chords in the given keys according to indicated degrees (T, S, D).

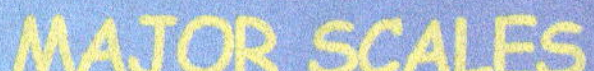

MAJOR SCALES

The **primary major scale** is the **C major scale**, which has **no key signature**. In addition to C major, there are **seven other major scales with sharps** and **seven more with flats**.

Major scales with sharps: G, D, A, E, B, F#, C#.
Major scales with flats: F, Bb, Eb, Ab, Db, Gb, Cb.

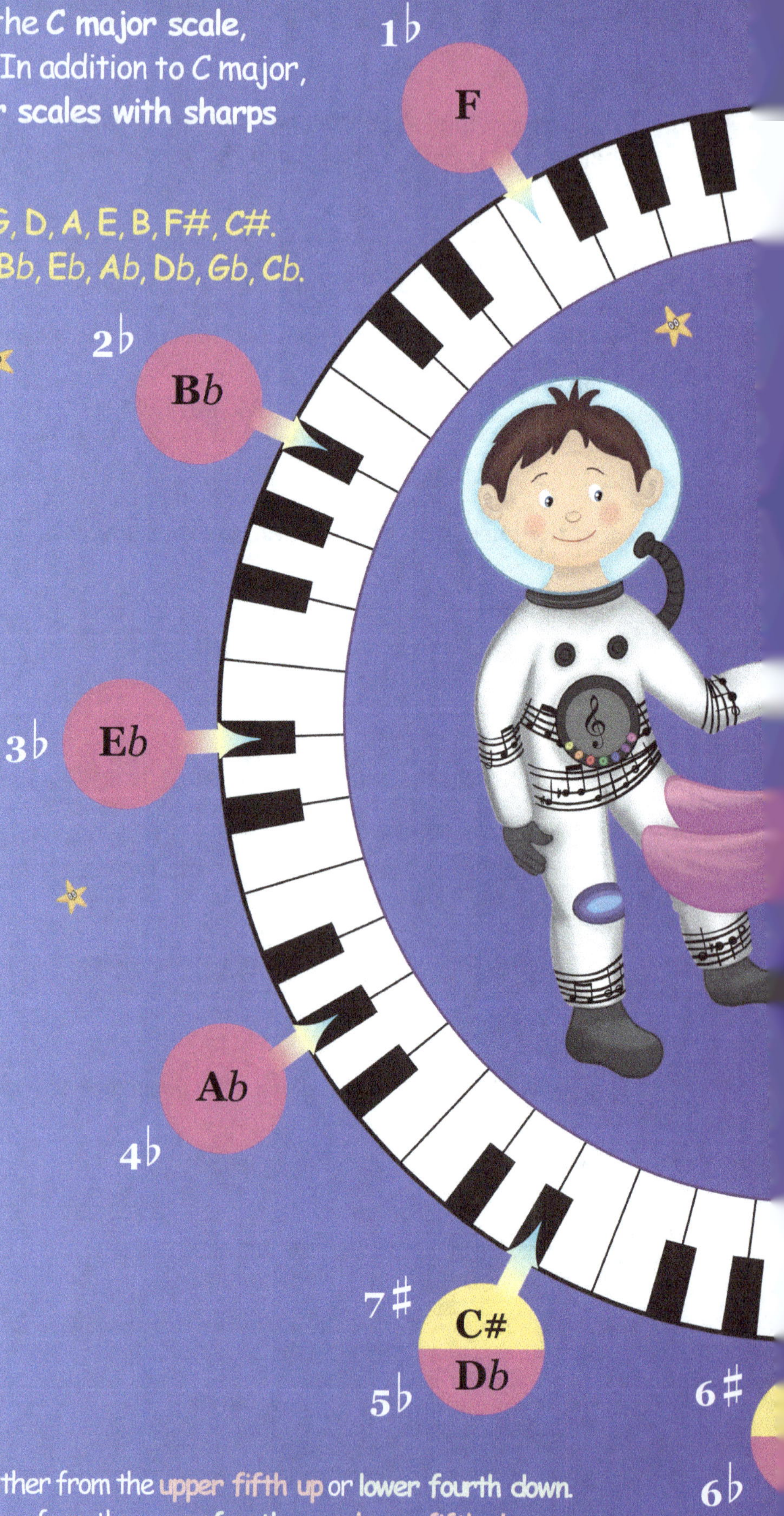

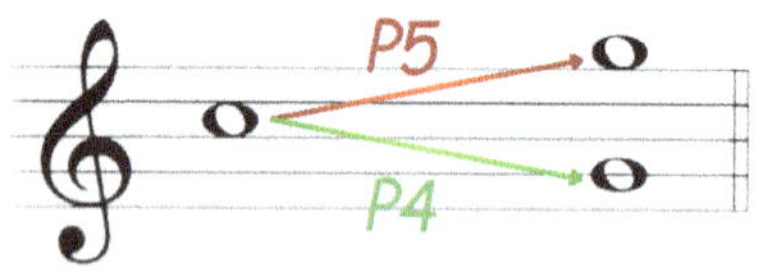

Scales with sharps:
P5 up or P4 down

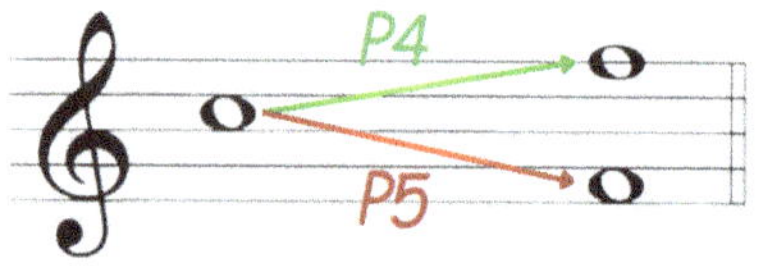

Scales with flats:
P4 up or P5 down

Major scales with sharps progress either from the **upper fifth up** or **lower fourth down**.
Major scales with flats progress either from the **upper fourth up** or **lower fifth down**.

CIRCLE OF FIIFTH
The progression of major scales with sharps and flats can be visualized as a circle. The scales are added in intervals of a 5th. Scales with sharps move in an ascending direction to the right (C–G–D–A…) and scales with flats descend to the left (C–F–Bb–Eb…).

1 #
G
2 #
D
A
2 #
E
4 #
B
Cb
5 #
7 b

Descending Fifths = Ascending Fourths
To simplify the learning process, descending fifths are often substituted with ascending fourths. Consequently, the major scales with flats can also be identified by moving in ascending perfect fourths.

Depending on the approach, Circle of Fifths is occasionally referred to as Circle of Fifths and/or Fourths.

MAJOR SCALES WITH FLATS

Major scales with flats follow the same basic rules as those with sharps. All major scales have a consistent pattern of whole steps and half steps - 1 1 1/2 1 1 1 1/2 . To keep this pattern unchanged across all major scales, we must adjust certain notes - raise or lower them. For major scales with flats, we do this by lowering the notes using **flats**.

MAJOR SCALES WITH FLATS
F major, Bb major, Eb major, Ab major, Db major, Gb major, Cb major

- Major scales with flats progress either on the **lower P5s** or their inversions **upper P4s**. We will focus on the ascending progression.
- The primary major scale is **C major**, which has **no key signature**.
- Each subsequent major scale with flats begins on the **lower P5** or **upper P4** of the previous scale.
- With each new scale, an additional **flat** is introduced on **its fourth degree**.
- The flats are added in this specific order: **Bb, Eb, Ab, Db, Gb, Cb**, and **Fb**.

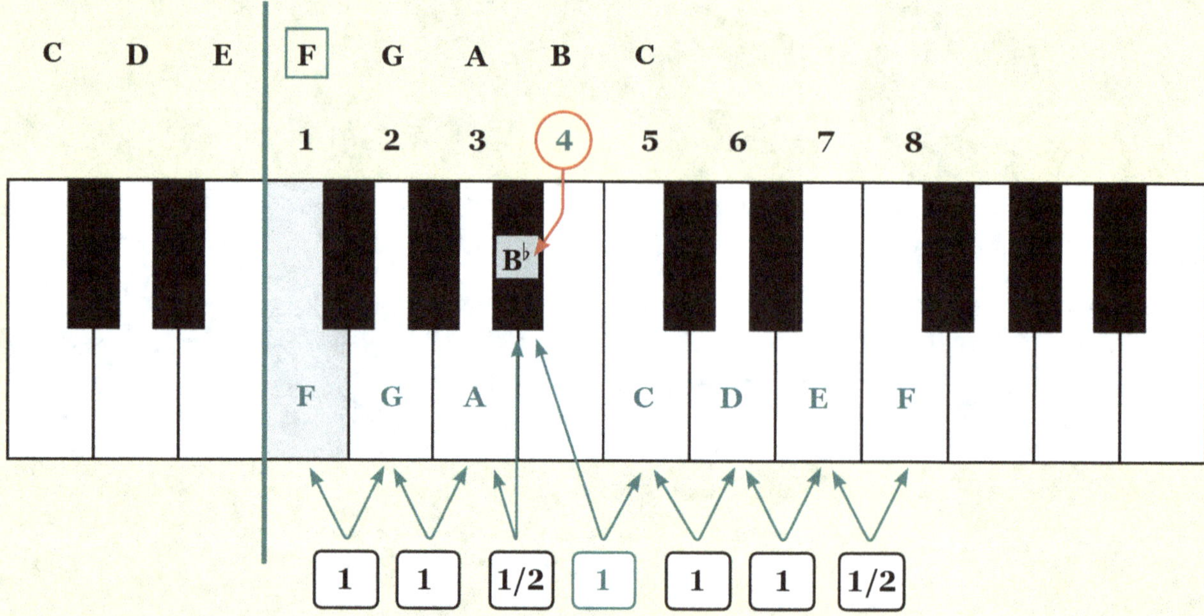

Example:
- *The scale with one flat starts on the lower fifth or upper fourth degree of the C major scale - the tone F.*
- *The F is the root tone of the new scale - the F major scale.*
- *Let's notate eight primary tones starting from the tone F up: F, G, A, B, C, D, E, F.*
- *To maintain the tone-half-tone major scale structure, we must lower new scale's fourth degree - B to Bb.*
- *The new scale, the F major scale, spells out F, G, A, Bb, C, D, E, F.*

E Notate the F major scale. Circle the note with the first flat in **green**.

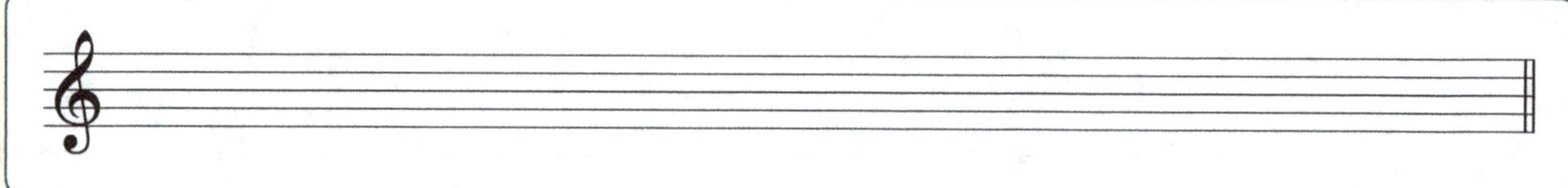

CIRCLE OF FIFTHS

The progression of the major scales with sharps and flats can be visualized in a closed circle.

- The scales with sharps are added clockwise by ascending P5s (C-G-D...).
- The scales with flats are added anti-clockwise by descending P5s (C-F-Bb...).

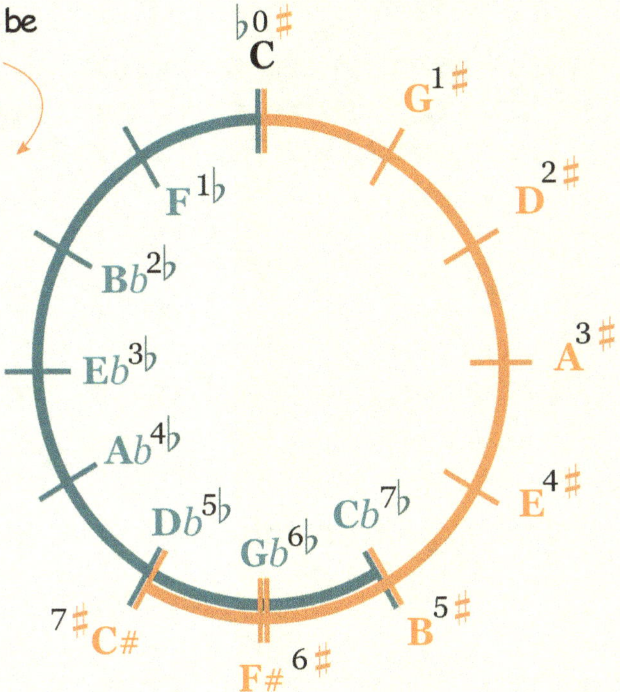

The scales meet and overlap at the bottom creating the complete circle.

Fascinating Facts about Scales with Sharps and Flats

The major scales featuring sharps and flats exhibit intriguing mirroring relationships. Within the Circle of Fifths, scales that possess an equal number of accidentals are positioned opposite each other, and there are additional related principles that come into play.

Sharps and Flats

- Sharps **raise** notes by a half-step.

- Flats **lower** notes by a half-step.

Key Signatures

- With scales with sharps, we raise the **7th degree of the new scale**.
- With scales with flats, we lower the **7th degree of the previous scale**.

Upper and Lower Intervals

- The scales with sharps progress by a sequence of **upper perfect fifths**.
- The scales with flats progress by a sequence of **lower perfect fifths**.

Lower Fifth = Upper Fourth

Upper fourth progressions are gradually replacing the instruction of lower fifth progressions to simplify learning.

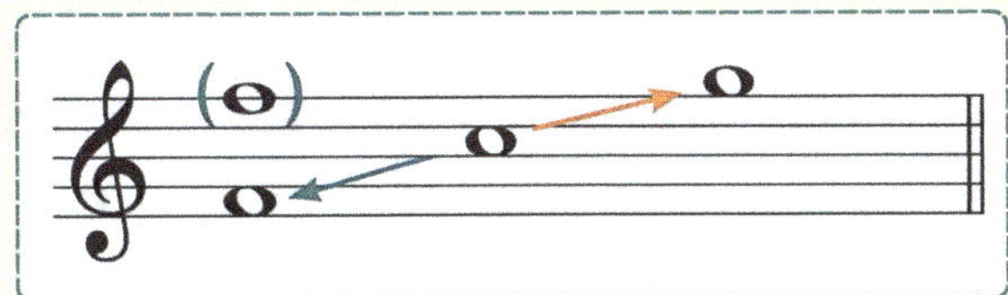

E Identify the intervals and write their abbreviated name on the lines below the measures.

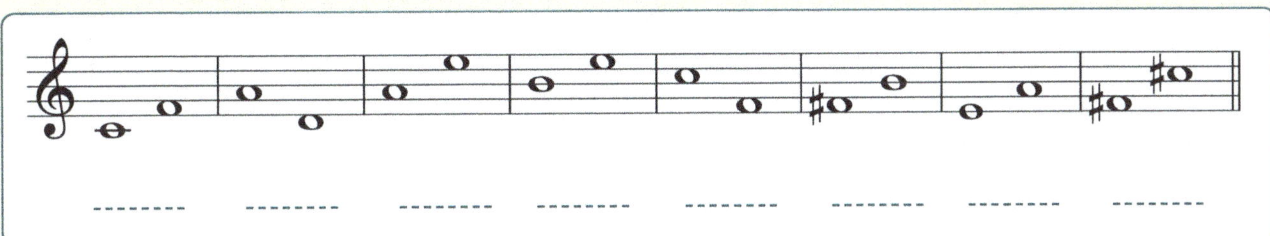

F MAJOR SCALE

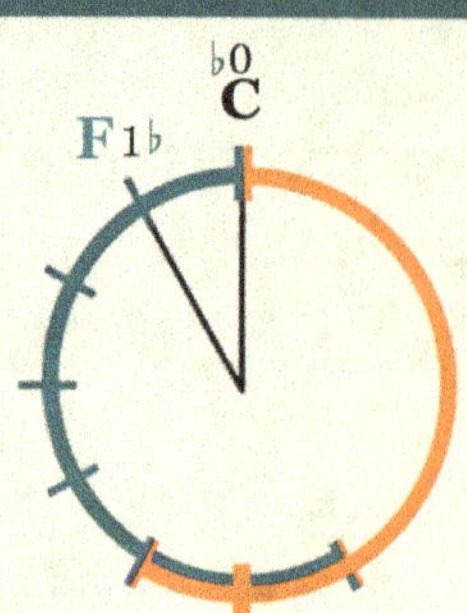

- The **F major** scale starts on the note **F**.
- **F** is the fourth degree of the primary **C** major scale.
- The major scales with flats: **F**, **Bb**, **Eb**, **Ab**, **Db**, **Gb**, **Cb**.

- The **F major tonic fifth chord** is **F-A-C** *(the 1st, 3rd, and 5th degrees)*. Its chord label is **F**.

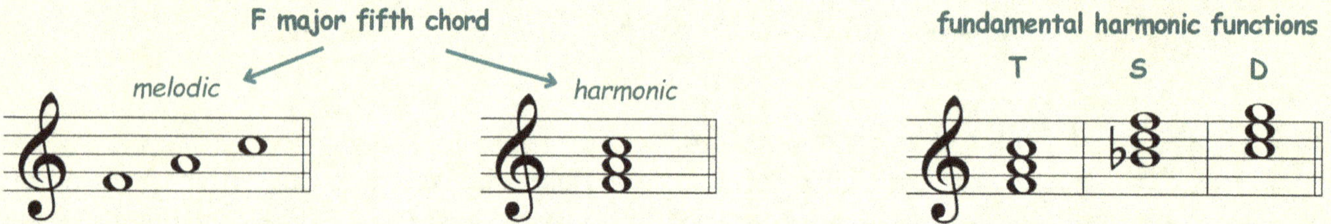

E | Notate the F major scale. Use brackets to identify the half-steps. Fill in the tonic fifth chord and its inversions. Pay attention to the chord symbols below the staff (see page 17).

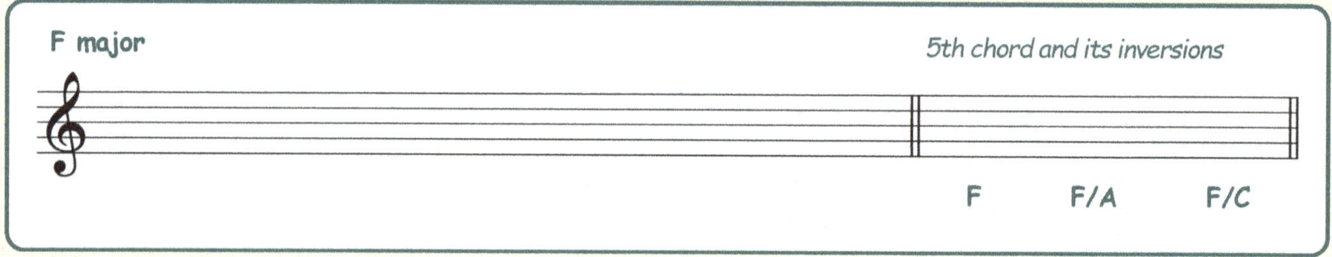

E | Learn the beautiful folk song below, then circle all the notes altered by the accidental.

B♭ MAJOR SCALE

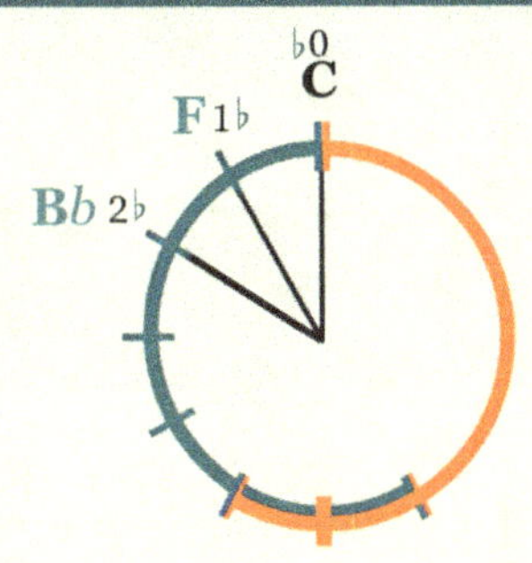

- The **B♭ major scale** starts on the note **B♭**.
- B♭ is the **fourth degree** of the F major scale.
- The major scales with flats: F, **B♭**, E♭, A♭, D♭, G♭, C♭.

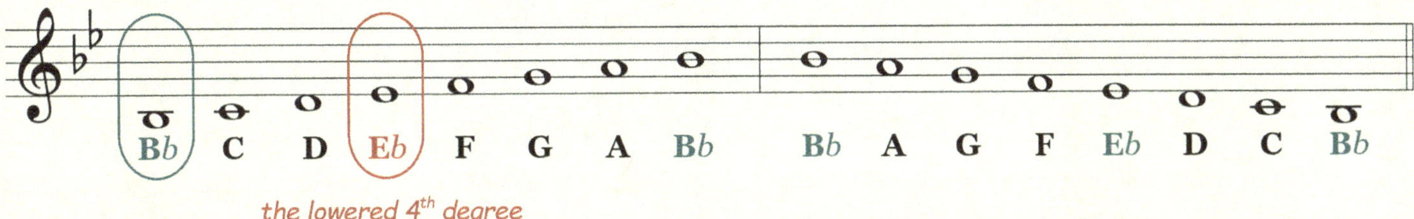

- The **B♭ major tonic fifth chord** is B♭-D-F *(the 1ˢᵗ, 3ʳᵈ, and 5ᵗʰ degrees)*. Its chord label is B♭.

E Fill in the B♭ major melodic and harmonic tonic fifth chords, its fundamental harmonic functions, the B♭ major scale *(use brackets to identify the half-steps)*, and the tonic fifth chord with its inversions.

E Learn the beautiful folk song below, then circle all the notes altered by the accidental.

E♭ MAJOR SCALE

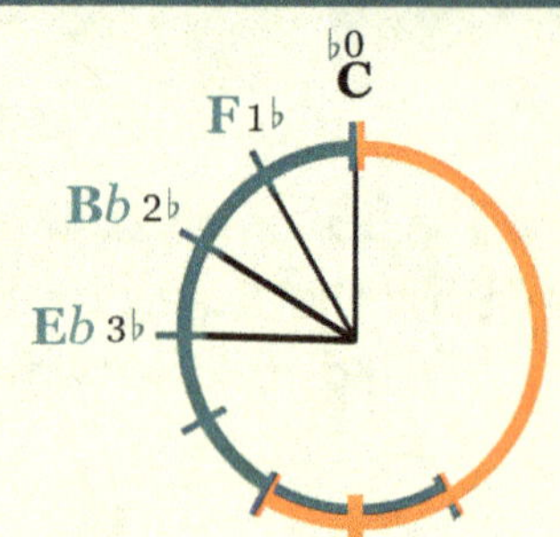

- The E♭ major scale starts on the note E♭.
- E♭ is the **fourth degree** of the B♭ major scale.
- The major scales with flats: F, B♭, E♭, A♭, D♭, G♭, C♭.

- The **E♭ major tonic fifth chord** is E♭-G-B♭ (*the 1ˢᵗ, 3ʳᵈ, and 5ᵗʰ degrees*). Its chord label is **E♭**.

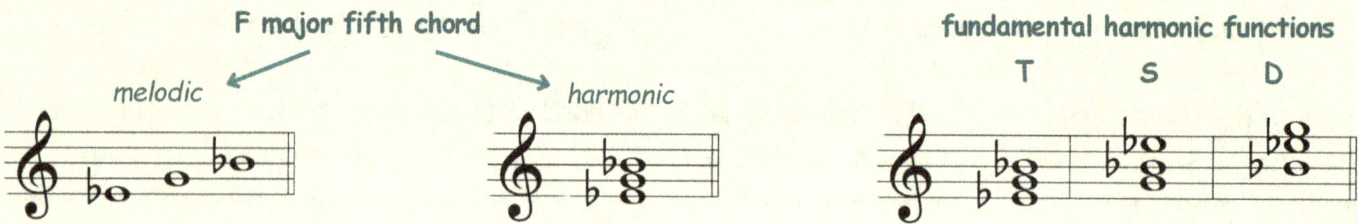

E Notate the E♭ major scale. Mark all the half stapes with brackets. Notate the tonic fifth chord and its inversions.

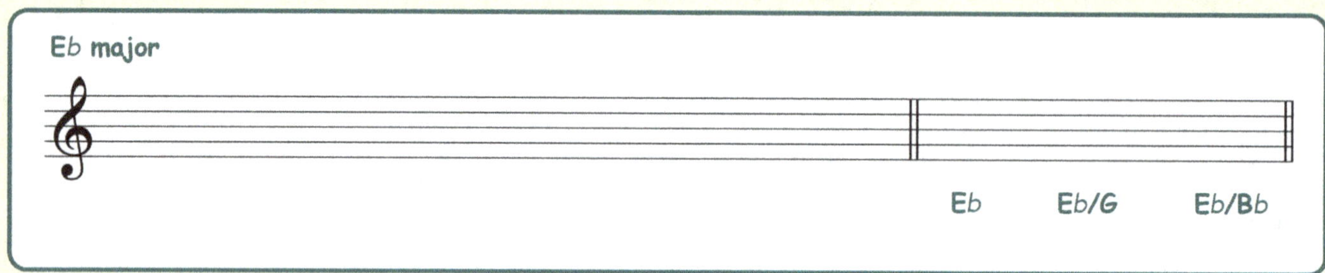

E Learn the song below. Review the upper and lower intervals. The song starts with the upper M3. Mark all the upper M3 intervals with brackets. In the song, you will encounter notation markings called "prima volta" and "seconda volta." The explanation of what they are and what they mean is on page 29.

Ab MAJOR SCALE

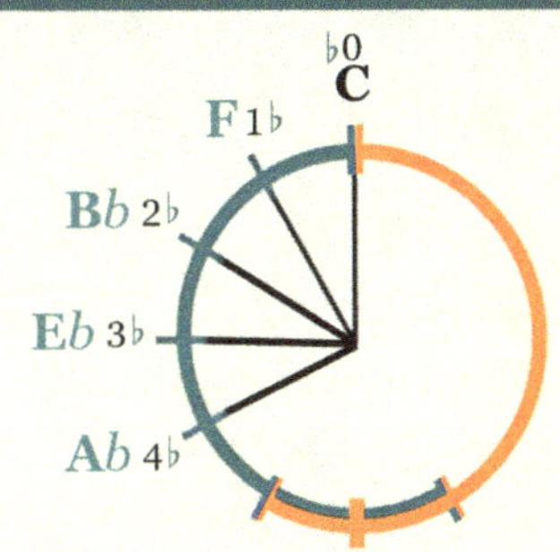

- The **Ab major scale** starts on the note **Ab**.
- **Ab** is the **fourth degree** of the Eb major scale.
- The major scales with flats: F, Bb, Eb, **Ab**, Db, Gb, Cb.

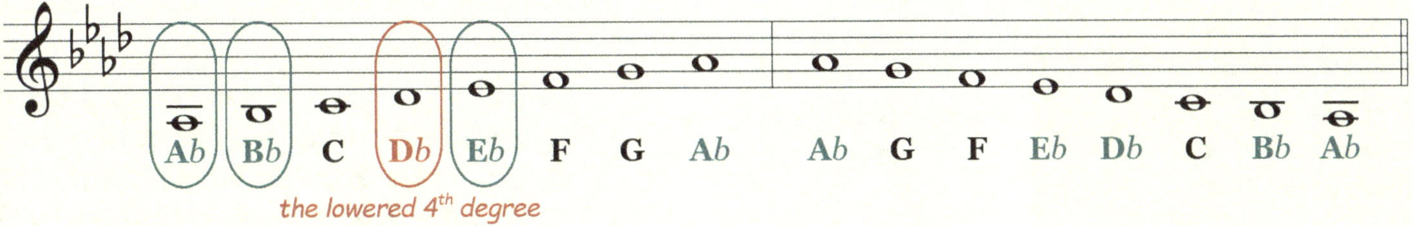

- The **Ab major tonic fifth chord** is **Ab-C-Eb** (the 1st, 3rd, and 5th degrees). Its chord label is **Ab**.

E Fill in the Ab major melodic and harmonic tonic fifth chords, its fundamental harmonic functions, the Ab major scale (*use brackets to identify the half-steps*), and the tonic fifth chord with its inversions.

E Learn the beautiful folk song below. Review the lower melodic m3 interval that appears in the song several times. Mark all the m3 intervals with brackets.

TEMPO MARKINGS

TEMPO MARKINGS

Slow Tempos

largo (*LAR-go*)   - broadly, very slow
adagio (*uh-DAH-jee-oh*)   - slow and stately
lento (*LEN-toe*)   - slowly, lengthy

Moderate Tempos

moderato (*MOD-er-AH-toe*)   - moderate, medium
andante (*on-DON-tay*)   - at a walking pace
andantino (*ON-don-TEE-noh*)   - at slightly faster walking pace
allegretto (*AL-luh-GRET-oh*)   - slightly fast

Fast Tempos

allegro (*uh-LAY-grow*)   - fast, lively, and happy
vivace (*vee-VAH-chay*)   - lively
vivo (*VEE-voh*)   - briskly
presto (*PRESS-toe*)   - very fast

TEMPO ALTERING MARKINGS

accelerando (*a-chel-er-AHN-do*) - gradually faster
ritardando (*ree-tar-DAHN-do*) - gradually slower
a tempo, tempo I (primo) - at initial tempo
fermata (*fr-MAA-tuh*) - sustain a note or a rest beyond its value

The tempo, which indicates the speed at which the piece should be performed, is located at the beginning of the composition, positioned above the staff.

E Match the tempo markings to their corresponding songs.

COMPOSITION TEMPO - meter

For a more precise understanding of tempo, we utilize meter. Meter indicates how many notes of a specific value should fit into a minute.

Example:

$$\text{♩} = 60$$

♩ 60 - 60 beats per minute
♩ - the beat is a quarter note

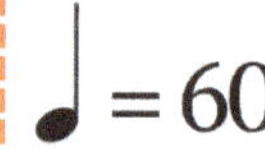

examples of tempo meters
largo = 44 beats
andante = 60 beats
allegro = 132 betas
presto 184 beats

Metronom

A metronome is a device that indicates tempo. It features a scale with tempo markings that allows users to set the speed of the beats. The first metronome was created in 1816 by the German musician Jan Mälzel.

NOTATION SIGNS

REPEAT SIGN

The repeat sign is a notation marking for repeating a marked section of a piece.
In case there is a different ending to a repeated section,
we use the following signs:

- **prima volta** = the first ending
- **seconda volta** = the second ending

DA CAPO (capo = Italian for "a head")

Da Capo (dah-KAH-poh), abbreviated **D.C.**, is a notation sign directing us to **repeat a piece from the beginning**.

- **D.C. al Fine** (dah KAH-poh ahl FEE-nay) = Repeat from the beginning until reaching the notation sign *fine* (fine = Italian for "an end"). Do not repeat any other sections; go directly to the *second volta* sections.
- **D.C. al Coda** (dah kah-poh ahl KOH-dah) = Repeat from the beginning
- until reaching the notation sign for Coda ⊕ and then go to the Coda section.

Coda (KOH-dah) is an Italian word meaning "a tail." In music, it is the name of an enriched concluding section of a piece. Its notation symbols look like this: ⊕

DAL SEGNO (segno = Italian for "a sign")

Dal Segno (dahl-SAY-nyoh), abbreviated **D.S.**, is a notation sign directing us to **repeat a piece from a symbol** that looks like this: 𝄋

- **D.S. al Fine** = Repeat from the sign 𝄋 to the end.
- **D.S. al Coda** = Repeat from the sign 𝄋, to the sign for Coda ⊕, then go to Coda.

*During the **initial play-through**, we play all the repeats and **prima voltas**. When **repeating**, we skip the repeats, do not play the prima voltas and proceed to the **seconda volta** sections if present. The same rule applies to all other repeat commands introduced in this chapter including **D.C. al Fine**, **D.C. al Coda**, **D.S. al Fine**, and **D.C. al Coda**.*

E Name all the signs for repetitions and endings. Sing or play the song, observing all the notation signs. Count the total number of measures and write it into the box.

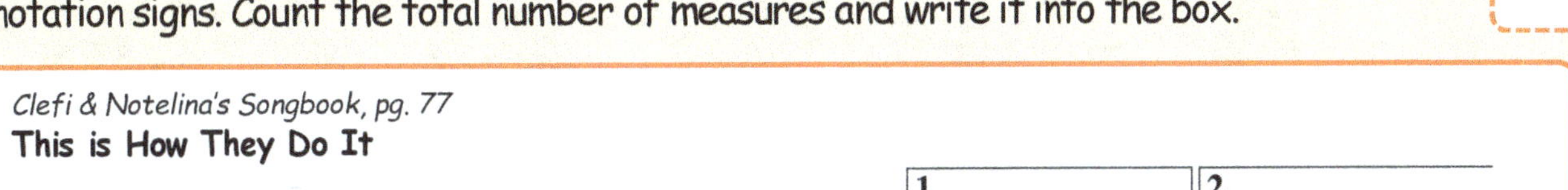

PICKUP MEASURE

PICKUP MEASURE or **ANACRUSIS** is an **incomplete measure** at the beginning of a composition. Occasionally, a composition begins with what is known as a **pickup measure** or **anacrusis**, which is essentially an **incomplete measure**. In this case, the final measure of the composition is usually also incomplete. Together, these two measures complement each other, as the combined number of beats in both incomplete measures equals the number of beats specified by the meter of the piece.

E Learn the song below.
Circle the pickup measure.

How many beats are in the anacrusis?
How many beats are in the lats measure?

E In the box, indicate the scale degree of the song's first note.
Transpose this section of the song into the keys of Eb, E, Ab, and A.

OCTAVE TRANSPOSITION

The **OCTAVE TRANSPOSITION** symbol is used in notation to avoid using too many ledger lines. The bass (F) and treble (G) clefs usually have enough space for all musical notes. However, to keep ledger lines to a minimum, we can use a special **octave transposition** symbol, which looks like this:

Octave transposition applies to **all notes within the bracket** of the symbol.
Depending on the position and direction of the bracket,
we can use this symbol for writing notes **sounding** an **octave higher** or **lower**.

The **musical alphabet** consists of seven fundamental tones: **C, D, E, F, G, A,** and **B.** This row of primary tones repeats several times at various pitches. The blocks created by these rows are called **octaves,** each identified by its **numeric** designation.

Complete Piano Keyboard

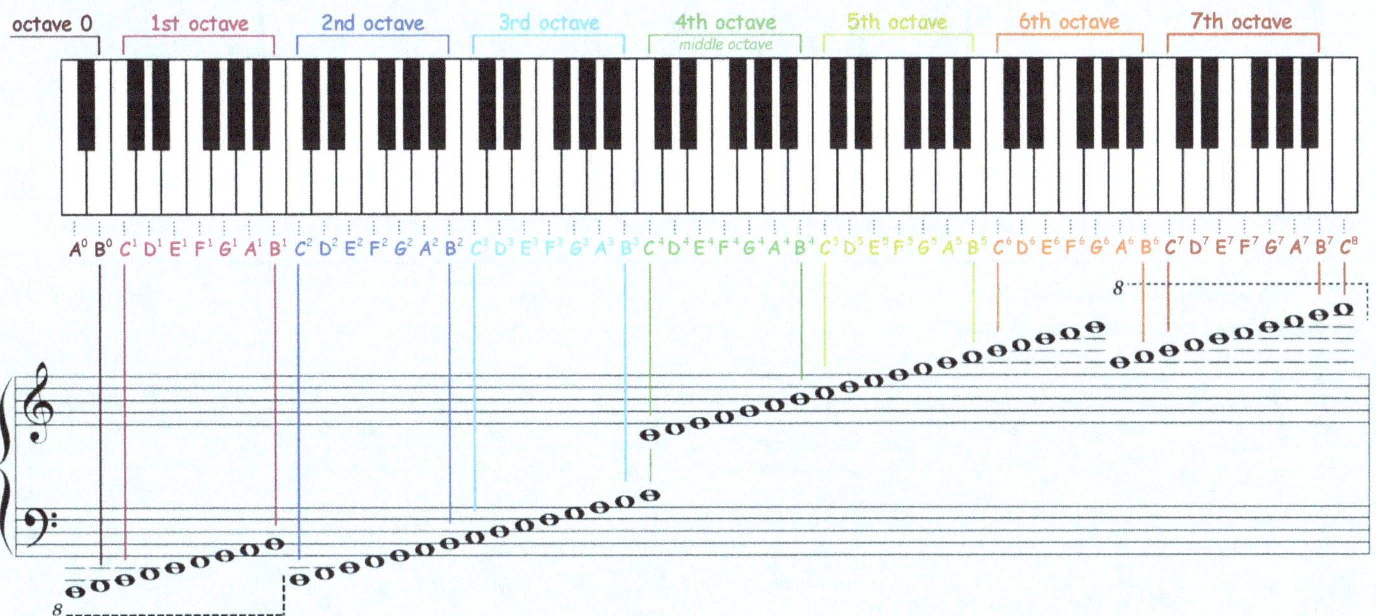

E Rewrite the section of the song with the use of the most suitable octave transposition sign.

ACCENT, SYNCOPATION

ACCENT

An **accent** accentuates a note, a group of notes, or a chord. Its most common musical symbol looks like an empty arrowhead placed above or below a note. When we see an accent, we are required to play or sing it. Accents can have different **levels of intensity**, shown by **various symbols**. Besides notated accents, there are naturally accented notes, such as downbeats and strong beats within a measure, which do not need to be marked with an accent.

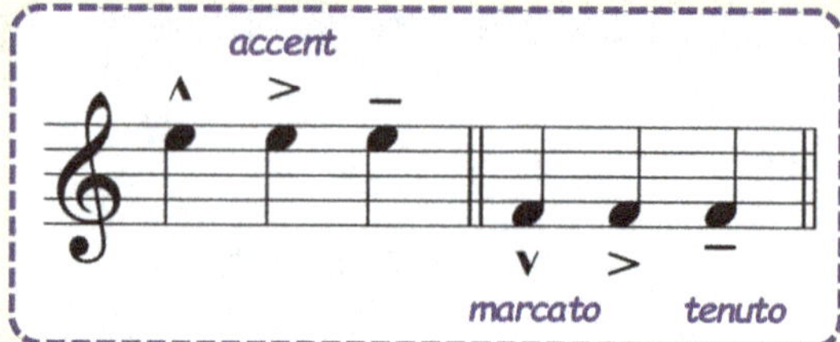

SYNCOPATION

The natural order of heavy and light beats within a measure can be rearranged, creating a cool **syncopated** rhythm. **Syncopation** is the transferring of a natural accent from a heavy beat to a light beat.

Example

Clefi & Notelina's Songbook, pg. 80
Hey, Mountain, Mountain Green

E Circle all the syncopations and write all the accents into the rhythmic notation of the song above.

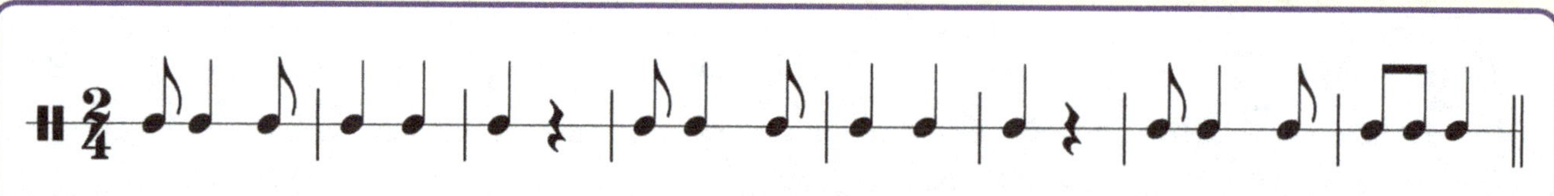

TRIPLET

TRIPLET

So far, we've explored how to break a note into **two shorter notes**: a whole note into two half notes, a half note into two quarter notes, and a quarter note into two eighth notes. However, it's also possible to divide a note into **three equal parts**, which we refer to as a *triplet*.

- In musical notation, a triplet is indicated by the number *3*.

Several ways a triplet can be indicated in notation:

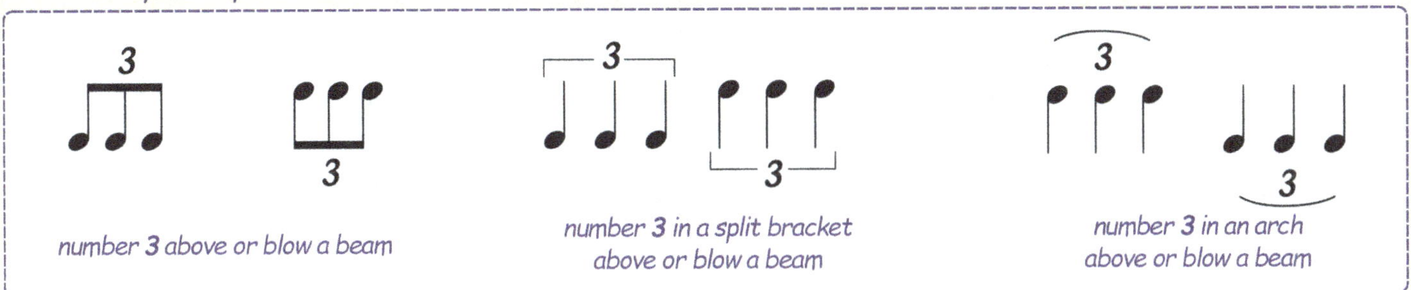

- Any note can be split into a triplet.

One triplet note equals one-third of the value of the subdivided note.

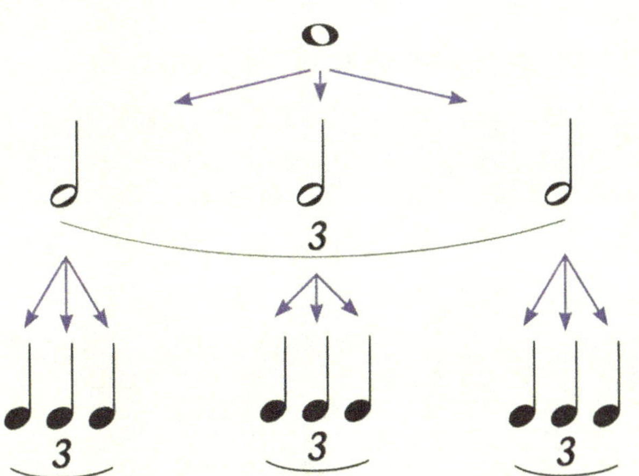

- The name of a triplet comes from the note values it contains.

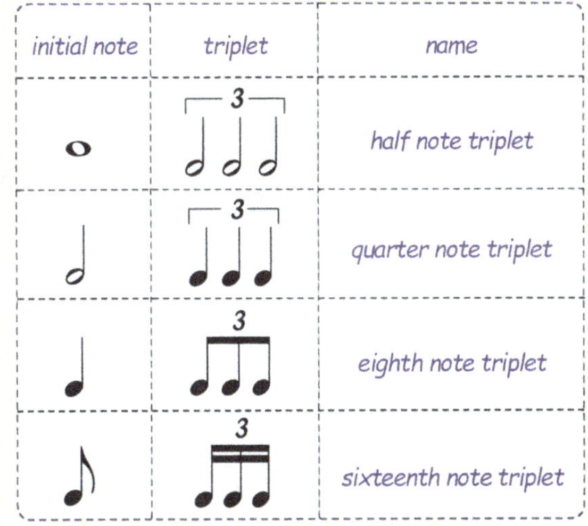

initial note	triplet	name
o	3	half note triplet
	3	quarter note triplet
	3	eighth note triplet
	3	sixteenth note triplet

To make sure the subdivision of a beat into a triplet is even when singing or playing it, we can sound it out like so: **trip-a-let, trip-a-let...**, or **one-and-a, two-and-a...**, or **pine-a-pple, pine-a-pple...**, etc.

E Clap the following rhythmical exercises, then clap the **beats** and **sound out** the **notes**.

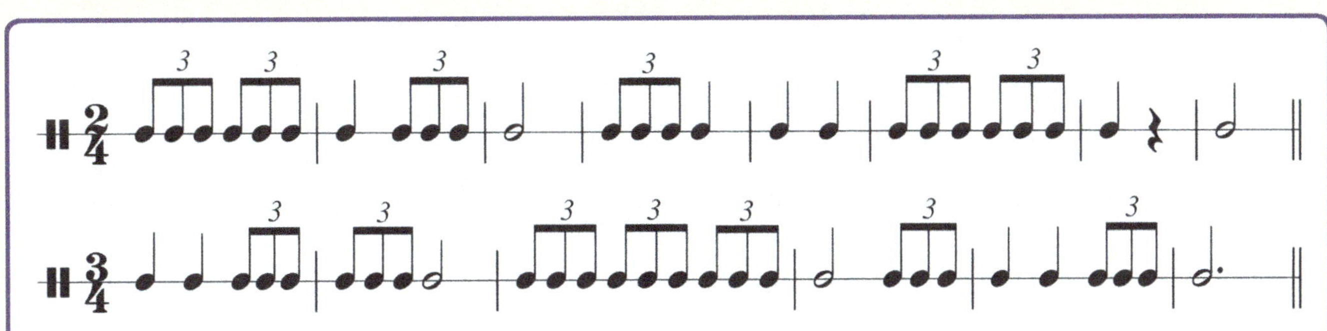

NOTATION

E Notate the notes by the assigned labels, using octave transposition symbols as needed.

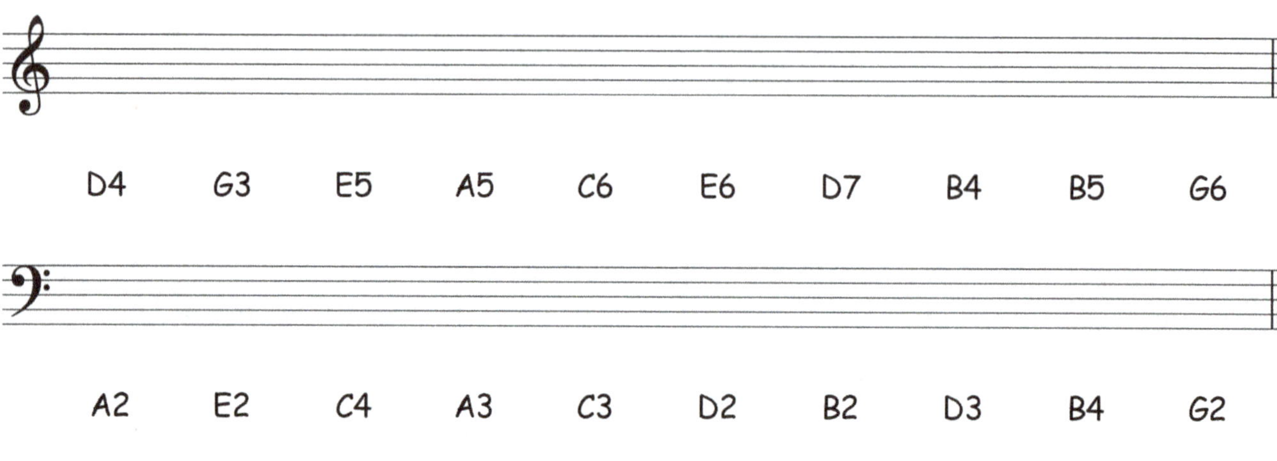

D4   G3   E5   A5   C6   E6   D7   B4   B5   G6

A2   E2   C4   A3   C3   D2   B2   D3   B4   G2

NOTATION

E Transpose the selected section of the song into the designated keys. Feel free to use key signatures or stand-alone accidentals as you see fit.   *Clefi & Notelina's Songbook, pg. 80*

F major

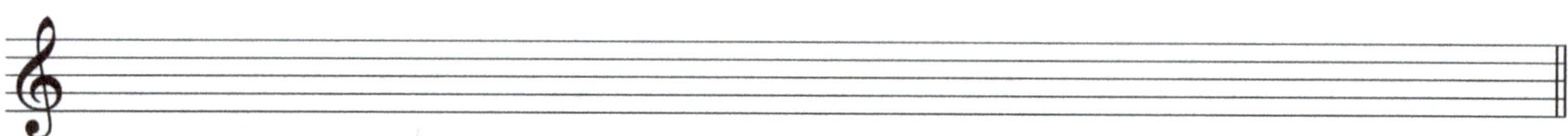

B♭ major

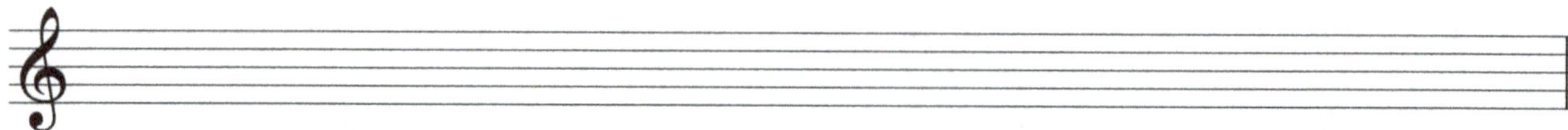

E♭ major

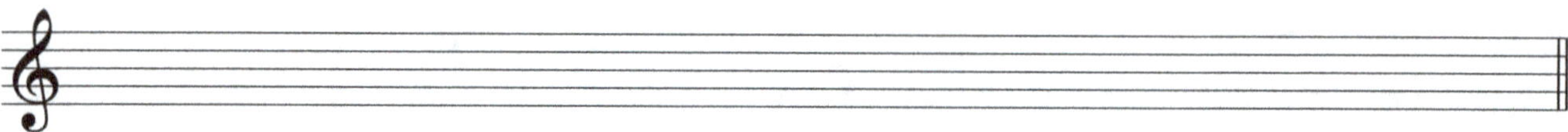

A♭ major

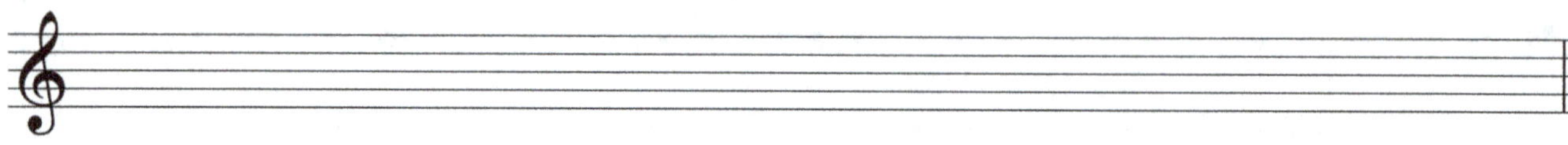

KEY SIGNATURES

E The opening of the song "I Used to Have a White Dove" starts on the 5th degree of its key.
Fill in the key signature into the box after the clef and name the key.
What do we call the incomplete measure at the beginning of the song? ....

Clefi & Notelina's Songbook, pg. 79

TEMPO MARKINGS

E Translate the tempo markings. Underline the slow tempos in red and fast tempos in green.

allegro   **largo**   **vivo**   **presto**   **adagio**   **lento**   **vivace**

RHYTHM - TRIPLETS, SYNCOPATION

E Clap the rhythmic exercises. Use red to circle the triplets and green for the syncopated
rhythms. What kind of triplets do you see?: ....

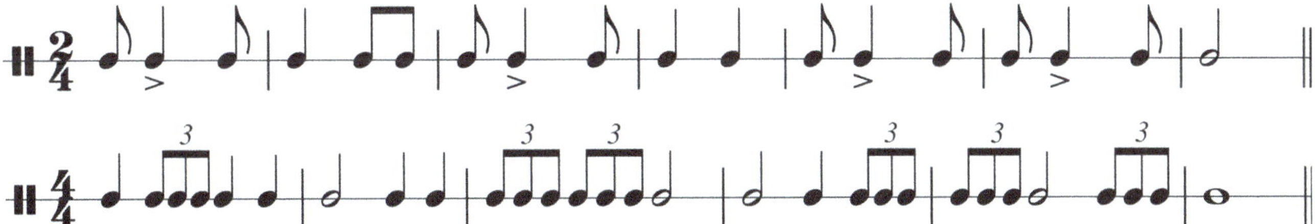

E Notate the correct quarter and eighth note triplets into the empty squares.

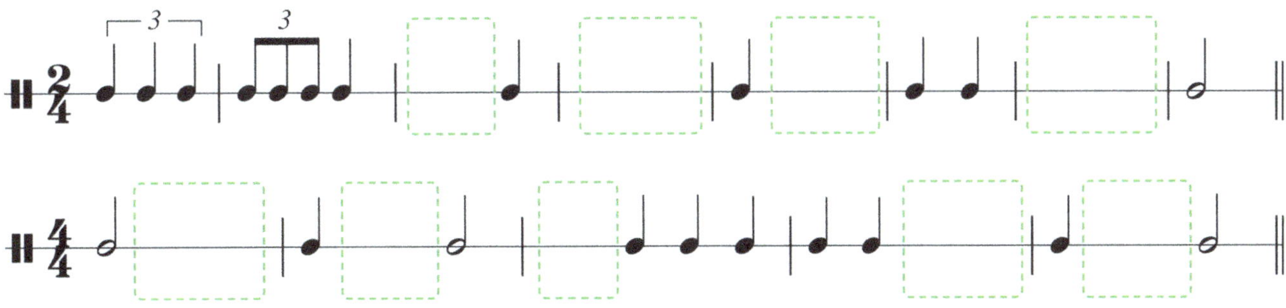

E Notate various rhythms in 4/4/ meter. Use half, quarter, and eighth note triplets.

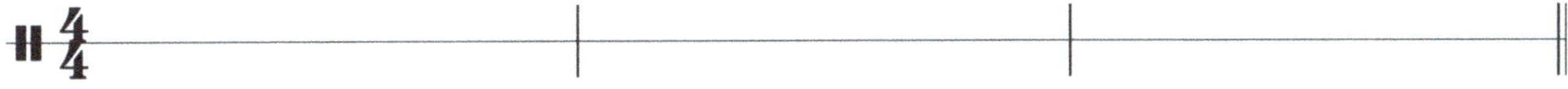

TONALITY

TONALITY - MODE

Tonality defines the overall character of keys and chords. It can be classified as either **major**, representing the **major mode**, or **minor**, representing the **minor mode**.

Tonal Character

When we listen to national folk songs, we can tell that some of them have a **happy** and some have a **sad character**.

Songs with a **happy, strong,** and **upbeat character** typically have **major tonality** = are in **major mode**, while those that sound **sad and melancholy** have **minor tonality** = are in **minor mode**. The tonality determines the **mood** of compositions.

Major Keys

- Major keys have **major tonality**.
- Their main characteristic is the **major third**.
- Major keys and modes are labeled using an **uppercase letter** (C = C major)
- Major tonic fifth chord contains M3 at the **bottom** and m3 at the **top**.

Minor Keys

- Minor keys have **minor tonality**.
- Their main characteristic is the **minor third**.
- Major keys and modes are labeled using an **uppercase letter** with "m" or "–" (**Cm** or **C-** = C minor) or sometimes **lowercase letter** (c = c minor).
- Major tonic fifth chord contains **m3 at the bottom** and **M3 at the top**.

Learn to sing or play the following beautiful Slovak national song that is written in the key of A minor. Its foundation is the minor fifth chord with m3 at the bottom - the main characteristic of minor modes.

Clefi & Notelina's Songbook, pg. 81
Good Night, My Sweet Love

E Identify both major and minor fifth chords. Highlight all major chords by circling them in red.

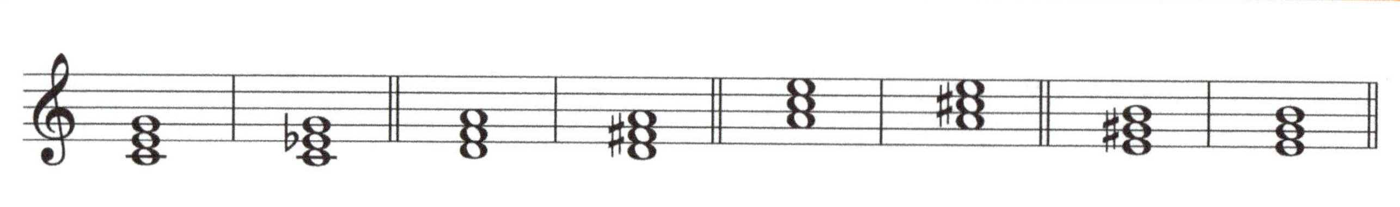

MINOR SCALE

RELATIVE SCALES

- Every major scale has its **relative minor scale** that contains the **same notes**. For example, the **C major** scale has the **same notes** as the **A minor** scale.
- Relative scales have the **same key signature**.
- A parallel minor scale starts on the **sixth degree** of its **relative major scale**.

Example:

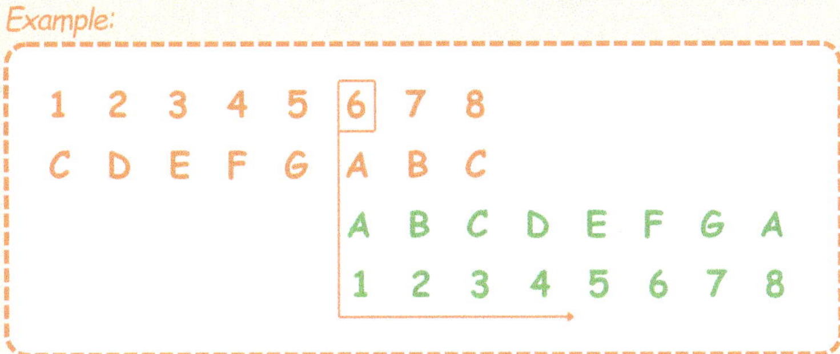

PRIMARY MINOR SCALE

- The primary minor scale is the **A minor scale**.
- The natural minor scale, which contains no altered tones, is called the **natural** or **Aeolian minor** scale.
- The A natural minor scale has **no key signature** and **no altered notes**.
- In the natural minor scale, **half steps** occur between the **2nd and 3rd** and the **5th and 6th** degrees.

Example:

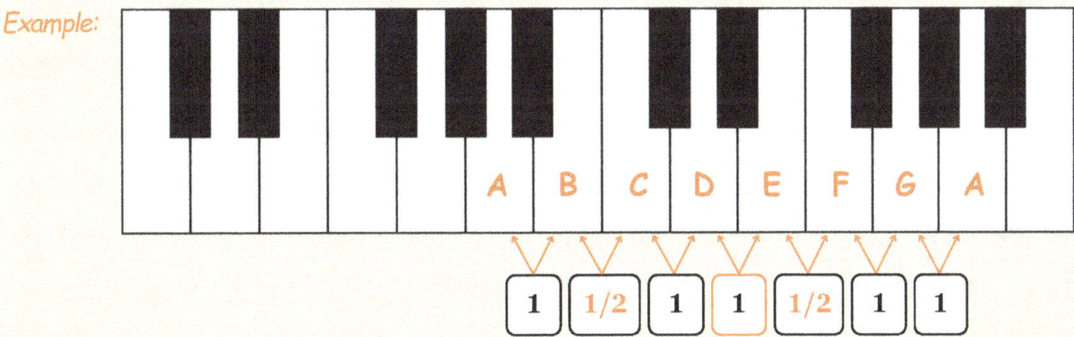

SCALE NAMES

The names of scales originates from their first note. Each scale is identified by the uppercase letter representing the first note, along with the appropriate accidental (either # or b), followed by the term "minor" or "major," as applicable.

E Mark half-steps and whole steps in the A minor scale. Verify your result with the piano keyboard. Then notate the A major scale and mark its half steps with red bracket. Compare both scales.

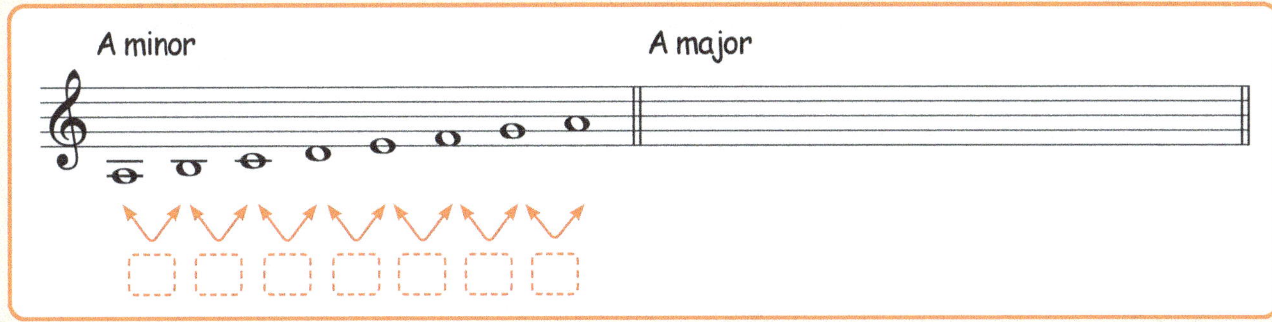

MINOR SCALES

In Western music, we use **three types** of minor scales:

Natural (Aeolian)
- Original minor scale with no altered tones.

Harmonic
- The seventh degree is raised in both ascending and descending motion.

Melodic
- When ascending, both the sixth and seventh degrees are raised, wile descending, the scale reverts to its natural form.

Natural Minor Scale

The natural minor scale is the **original minor scale**.

Natural A minor

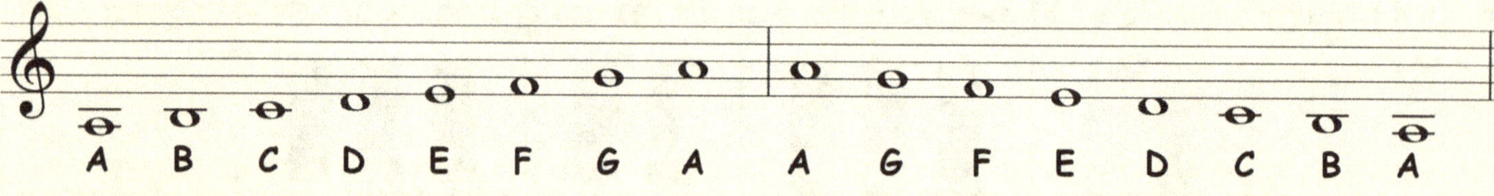

Harmnoic Minor Scale (raised 7th degree)

The harmonic minor scale has the same notes as the natural minor except for the **raised seventh degree in both directions**. The seventh degree is altered using an **accidental** - a sharp or a natural.

Harmonic A minor

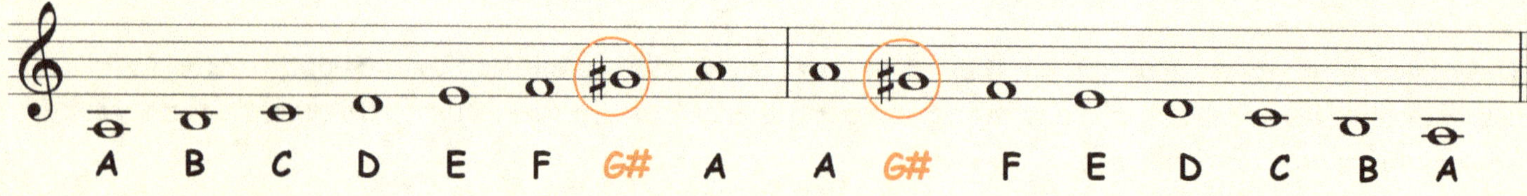

Melodic Minor Scale (raised 6th and 7th degrees ascending, same as the natural minor descending)

The melodic minor scale has the same notes as the natural minor except for the **raised sixth and seventh degrees in ascending** motion. **When descending**, the scale reverts to its **natural form**. To alter the notes, we use **accidentals**.

Melodic A minor

DEVELOPMENT OF THE MINOR SCALE

The natural minor scale does not include the **leading tone** - the major seventh. While listening to compositions and singing songs, we experience our natural need to use the pull of the leading tone toward the foundational tone—the tonic. However, the natural minor scale does not provide this.

The harmonic minor scale addresses this issue by raising the seventh degree, **creating the M7 interval** and, consequently, the **leading tone**. However, this adjustment results in the **augmented second interval** - the **1½ step** - between the sixth and seventh degrees. Such an interval **does not sound very melodic** to our Western-music-trained ears. And so, the search for another solution continued.

The melodic minor scale is here to satisfy our longing for **beautiful minor melodies**. With its raised sixth and seventh degrees in ascending motion, it **offers** the coveted **leading tone** and **eliminates the augmented second** present in the harmonic scale.

Key Features of Minor Scales

- **Natural minor scales** have half steps between the 2nd and 3rd, and the 5th and 6th degrees.
- **Harmonic minor scales** include the interval of augmented second, which skips 1½ steps between the 6th and 7th degrees. This distinctive skip is easily identifiable by ear and is labeled as **+2** or **A2**.
- **Melodic minor scales** differ when ascending and when descending. In the ascending motion, the first tetrachord sounds minor and the second major.

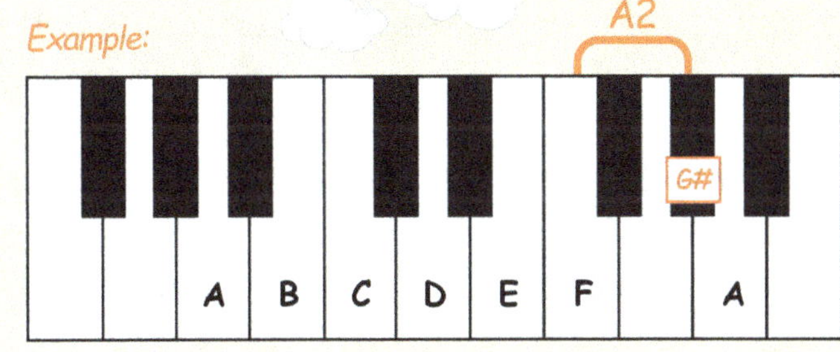

Harmonic minor scale featuring the uncommon skip, the interval of +2 or A2 (1½ steps).

E   Notate A harmonic minor scale. Mark the uncommon skip of 1½ steps between the 6th and 7th degrees in red. Practice recognizing the M2 (a whole step) and A2 (1½ steps). Circle all the A2 intervals in red.

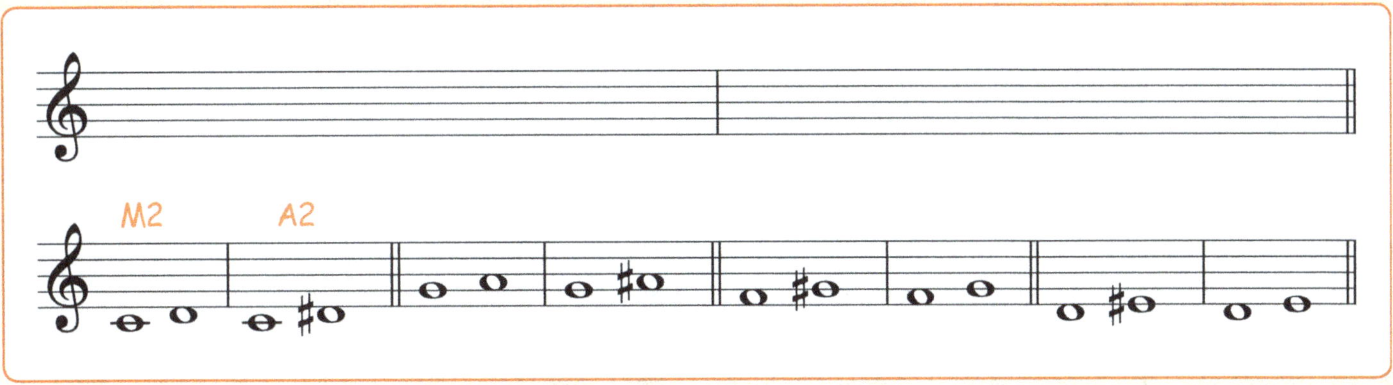

E   Notate A melodic minor scale. Label each note beneath the staff, and circle the notes that differ between the ascending and descending motions of the scale

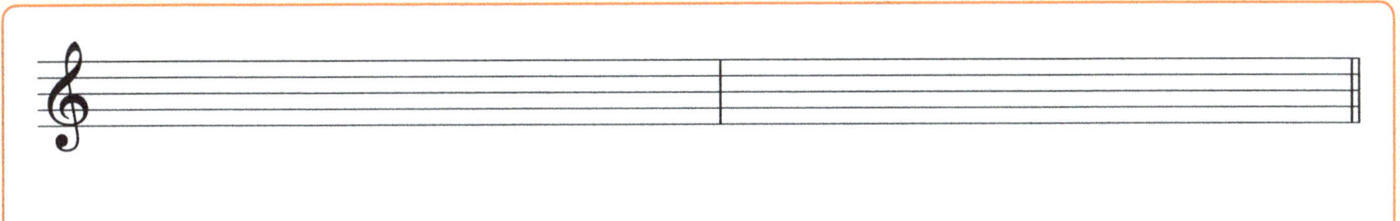

TUNING

Pythagoras's Quest for Pure Pitch

Three thousand years ago, music was a source of joy, with people singing and playing for enjoyment. During this era, ancient Greece stood as the hub of European culture. For the elite in ancient Greek society, a well-rounded education included not just literacy, but also knowledge in both the sciences and the arts.

During that time, people played music as a solo. Instruments were used to play either a melodic line or accompany singing. Ensemble playing was not practiced. They used melodic and stringed instruments, such as the lyre or harp, for playing only melodies. But then they started playing together, creating harmonies (multiple notes played simultaneously) or using multiple instruments that played in unison, which caused tuning issues. Performances had to stay within the range of one octave. When musicians played over a wider range, the high tones would sound out of tune with the lower ones.

The first person to attempt solving this tuning problem was the **Greek philosopher** and **scholar Pythagoras**, who lived in the 6th century BC. To study tones, he used a single-string instrument called a **monochord**.

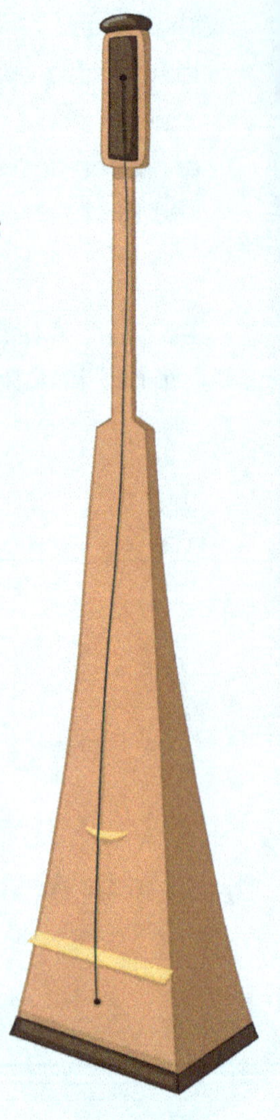

Monochord

Pythagoras was a musician, a scholar, a mathematician, and a physicist. Thanks to his knowledge of physical laws, he discovered that if you split a vibrating string in half by touching it in the middle, the string produces a tone an octave higher than the open string. In this way, he discovered the laws of string vibrations that affect pitch. This became the foundation for the theory of tuning and musical intervals. He derived these laws from natural tuning, and he modified this natural tuning so that instruments could be tuned to play together in harmony. He invented a tuning system called **Pythagorean tuning**. But it was not to last.

While this system was better than natural tuning, it later became unsuitable when polyphonic instruments (like the piano or organ) were invented. People struggled with tuning until the **16th century**, when a solution was found. This solution was so-called **equal temperament tuning**, which is still used today. Thanks to the equal temperament tuning, instruments can now be tuned across all octaves so that harmonies sound in tune. However, the natural tuning did not completely vanish. The natural unison and the octave were preserved. The remaining tones were divided into 12 equal parts and fit between the unison and the octave. The intervals of fourth and fifth remained nearly identical to their natural tuning origins. Even after the slight adjustment imposed on them by the equal temperament tuning, our ears still perceive them as natural, pure, or **perfect**. Therefore, the labeling of these intervals is not just a chance or coincidence. **Unison**, **fourth**, **fifth**, and **octave** are called **perfect intervals** for a historic reason.

CERTIFICATE

OF COMPLETION

This certificate is presented to:

For successfully completing
Clefi's Music Notebook 2

music education teacher

Clefi's and Notelina's
Little American-British-International Music Dictionary

Music is a universal language; that is true. However, every nation uses its own beautiful tongue to describe and teach music. Clefi is originally Klíček, a little Czech boy who guides children through the fundamentals of music theory using the Czech language and music terminology. His American twin brother Clefi had to translate and adapt the text so English-speaking children could enjoy the journey. However, not all English-speaking musicians use the same music terms. Therefore, Clefi created this little American-British Music Dictionary of music terms used in this book to accommodate our British English-speaking music friends.

General Music Terms

Staff *(Staffs)*	**Stave** *(Staves)*
Grand staff	**Great stave**
Measure, measure line	**Bar, Barline**
Fermata	**Pause, Hold**

Octaves

Zero octave	**Sub-contra octave**
First octave	**Contra octave**
Second octave	**Great octave**
Thirds octave	**Small octave**
Fourth (middle) **octave**	**One-line octave**
Fifth octave	**Two-line octave**
Sixth octave	**Three-line octave**
Seventh octave	**Four-line octave**

Note Distances

Whole step	**Tone**
Half step	**Semitone**

Notes

C1-B1	**C, (contra) - B, (contra)**
C2-B2	**C (great) - B (great)**
C3-B3	**c (small) - b (small)**
C4-B4 (middle)	**c'-b'** (one-line c - 1 line b)
C5-B5	**c"-b"** (two-line c - 2 line b)
C6-B6	**c'''-b'''** (three-line c - 3 line b)
C7-B7	**Cc''''-b''''** (four-line c - 4 line b)

Note Values

Double whole note *(rest)*	**Breve** *(rest)*
Whole note *(rest)*	**Semibreve** *(rest)*
Half note *(rest)*	**Minim** *(rest)*
Quarter note *(rest)*	**Crotchet** *(rest)*
Eighth note *(rest)*	**Quaver** *(rest)*
Sixteenth note *(rest)*	**Semiquaver** *(rest)*
Thirty-second note	**Demisemiquaver** *(rest)*
Sixty-fourth note	**Hemidemisemiquaver** *(rest)*

Intervals

Across continental Europe, the rich musical tradition has led most countries to adopt Italian names for numerous musical symbols and terms, particularly for intervals. While we could provide a detailed comparison with country-specific translations and adaptations, we believe it's more effective to engage your musical intuition. Therefore, we invite you to explore the beauty and expressiveness of music by focusing solely on the Italian names of the most commonly used intervals. Embrace this journey and let your imagination resonate whenever you encounter a musical friend from another country!.

Unison .... Prima
Second .... Seconda
Third .... Terza
Fourth .... Quarta
Fifth .... Quinta
Sixth .... Sesta
Seventh .... Settima
Octave .... Ottava
Ninth .... Nona
Tenth .... Decima
Eleventh .... Undicesima
Twelfth .... Dodicesima

One Final Question

What single musical term comes to your mind when you look at the pictures below? in the pictures below? Write it in the box.

Answer Key to
Clefi's Little
Crossword Review

Down:

1. A part off an eight note.
2. The distance between C and D.
3. The one-beat rest.
4. C4.
6. The primary scale.
7. Musical symbols for tones.
10. The grid used for musical notation.
11. The major scale with the most sharps.
14. The four parts of the musical staff.
15. A two-beat note.
20. Musical symbols for silence in music.
23. The five parts of the musical staff.

Across:

5. The treble clef.
8. A four-beat note.
9. A combination of three or more notes.
12. Small sections of musical notation.
13. The distance between E and F.
16. The names of tone and notes.
17. The canceling accidental.
18. The difference between two pitches.
19. The altered note F.
21. The vertical line attached to shorter notes.
22. F clef.
24. The line connecting several eighth notes.